Bible Interpretations

Fifteenth Series
January 6-March 31, 1895

Mathew, Mark, Luke, John and Romans

Bible Interpretations

Fifteenth Series

Mathew, Mark, Luke, John and Romans

These Bible Interpretations were published in the Inter-Ocean Newspaper in Chicago, Illinois during the late eighteen nineties.

By
Emma Curtis Hopkins

President of the Emma Curtis Hopkins Theological Seminary at Chicago, Illinois

WISEWOMAN PRESS

Bible Interpretations: Fifteenth Series
By Emma Curtis Hopkins

© WiseWoman Press 2013
Managing Editor: Michael Terranova

ISBN: 978-0945385-66-0

WiseWoman Press
Vancouver, WA 98665

www.wisewomanpress.com
www.emmacurtishopkins.com

CONTENTS

	Foreword by Rev. Natalie R. Jean ix
	Introduction by Rev. Michael Terranova xi
I.	Missing 1
	Mark 6:17-29 Jan 6, 1895
II.	The Prince Of The World 3
	Mark 6:30-44
III.	Comments and Explanations on The Golden Text 13
	John 6:25-35
IV.	Comments and Explanations on The Golden Text 27
	Matthew 16:13-25
V.	The Transfiguration 39
	Luke 9:28-36
VI.	Christ And The Children 49
	Matthew 18:1-14
VII.	The Good Samaritan 61
	Luke 10:25-37
VIII.	Christ And The Man Born Blind 71
	John 9:1-11
IX.	The Raising Of Lazarus 83
	John 11:30-45
X.	The Rich Young Ruler 93
	Mark 10:17-27
XI.	Zaccheus The Publican 103
	Luke 1:10
XII.	Purity Of Life 115
	Romans 13:8-14
XIII.	Review 127
	List of Bible Interpretation Series 142

Editors Note

All lessons starting with the *Seventh Series of Bible Interpretations* are Sunday postings from the Inter-Ocean Newspaper in Chicago, Illinois. Many of the lessons in the following series were retrieved from the International New Thought Association Archives, in Mesa, Arizona by, Rev Joanna Rogers. Many others were retrieved from libraries in Chicago, and the Library of Congress, by Rev. Natalie Jean.

All the lessons follow the Sunday School Lesson Plan published in "Peloubet's International Sunday School Lessons." The passages to be studied are selected by an International Committee of traditional Bible Scholars.

Some of Emma's lessons don't have a title. In these cases the heading will say "Comments and Explanations of the Golden Text," followed by the Bible passages to be studied.

Foreword

By Rev. Natalie R. Jean

I have read many teachings by Emma Curtis Hopkins, but the teachings that touch the very essence of my soul are her Bible Interpretations. There are many books written on the teachings of the Bible, but none can touch the surface of the true messages more than these Bible interpretations. With each word you can feel and see how Spirit spoke through Emma. The mystical interpretations take you on a wonderful journey to Self Realization.

Each passage opens your consciousness to a new awareness of the realities of life. The illusions of life seem to disappear through each interpretation. Emma teaches that we are the key that unlocks the doorway to the light that shines within. She incorporates ideals of other religions into her teachings, in order to understand the commonalities, so that there is a complete understanding of our Oneness. Emma opens our eyes and mind to a better today and exciting future.

Emma Curtis Hopkins, one of the Founders of New Thought teaches us to love ourselves, to speak our Truth, and to focus on our Good. My life has moved in wonderful directions because of her teachings. I know the only thing that can move me in this world is God. May these interpretations guide you to a similar path and may you truly remember that "There Is Good For You and You Ought to Have It."

Introduction

Emma Curtis Hopkins was born in 1849 in Killingsly, Connecticut. She passed on April 8, 1925. Mrs. Hopkins had a marvelous education and could read many of the worlds classical texts in their original language. During her extensive studies she was always able to discover the Universal Truths in each of the world's sacred traditions. She quotes from many of these teachings in her writings. As she was a very private person, we know little about her personal life. What we do know has been gleaned from other people or from the archived writings we have been able to discover.

Emma Curtis Hopkins was one of the greatest influences on the New Thought movement in the United States. She taught over 50,000 people the Universal Truth of knowing "God is All there is." She taught many of the founders of early New Thought, and in turn these individuals expanded the influence of her teachings. All of her writings encourage the student to enter into a personal relationship with God. She presses us to deny anything except the Truth of this spiritual Presence in every area of our lives. This is the central focus of all her teachings.

The first six series of Bible Interpretations were presented at her seminary in Chicago, Illinois. The remaining Series, probably close to thirty, were printed in the Inter Ocean Newspaper in Chicago. Many of the lessons are no longer available for various reasons. It is the intention of WiseWoman Press to publish as many of these Bible Interpretations as possible. Our hope is that any missing lessons will be found or directed to us.

I am very honored to join the long line of people that have been involved in publishing Emma Curtis Hopkins's Bible Interpretations. Some confusion exists as to the numbering sequence of the lessons. In the early 1920's many of the lessons were published by the Highwatch Fellowship. Inadvertently the first two lessons were omitted from the numbering system. Rev. Joanna Rogers has corrected this mistake by finding the first two lessons and restoring them to their rightful place, in the order written. Rev. Rogers has been able to find many of the missing lessons at the International New Thought Alliance archives in Mesa, Arizona. Rev. Rogers painstakingly scoured the archives for the missing lessons as well as for Mrs. Hopkins other works. She has published much of what was discovered. WiseWoman Press is now publishing the correctly numbered series of the Bible Interpretations.

In the early 1940's, there was a resurgence of interest in Emma's works. At that time, Highwatch Fellowship began to publish many of her writings, and it was then that *High Mysticism*, her seminal work was published. Previously, the material contained in High Mysticism was only available as individual lessons and was brought together in book form for at that time. Although there were many errors in these first publications and many Bible verses were incorrectly quoted, I am happy to announce that WiseWoman Press is now publishing *High Mysticism* in the correct format. This corrected form was scanned faithfully from the original, individual lessons.

The next person to publish some of the Bible Lessons was Rev. Marge Flotron of the Ministry of Truth International in Chicago, Illinois. She published the Bible Lessons as well as many of Emma's other works. By her initiative, Emma's writings were brought to a larger audience when DeVorss & Company, a longtime publisher of Truth teachings, took on the publication of Emma's key works.

In addition, Dr. Carmelita Trowbridge, founding minister of The Sanctuary of Truth in Alhambra, California, inspired her assistant minister, Rev. Shirley Lawrence, to publish many of Emma's works, including the first three series of Bible Interpretations. Rev. Lawrence created mail order courses for many of these

Series. She has graciously passed on any information she had, in order to assure that these works continue to inspire individuals and groups who are called to further study of the teachings of Mrs. Hopkins.

Finally, a very special acknowledgement goes to Rev Natalie Jean, who has worked diligently to retrieve several of Emma's lessons from the Library of Congress, as well as libraries in Chicago. Rev. Jean hand-typed many of the lessons she found on microfilm. Much of what she found is on her website, www.highwatch.net.

It is with a grateful heart that I am able to pass on these wonderful teachings. I have been studying dear Emma's works for fifteen years. I was introduced to her writings by my mentor and teacher, Rev. Marcia Sutton. I have been overjoyed with the results of delving deeply into these Truth Teachings.

In 2004, I wrote a Sacred Covenant entitled "Resurrecting Emma," and created a website, www.emmacurtishopkins.com. The result of creating this covenant and website has brought many of Emma's works into my hands and has deepened my faith in God. As a result of my love for these works, I was led to become a member of WiseWoman Press and to publish these wonderful teachings. God is Good.

My understanding of Truth from these divinely inspired teachings keeps bringing great Joy, Freedom, and Peace to my life.

Dear reader; It is with an open heart that I offer these works to you, and I know they will touch you as they have touched me. Together we are living in the Truth that God is truly present, and living for and through each of us.

The greatest Truth Emma presented to us is "My Good is my God, Omnipresent, Omnipotent and Omniscient."

Rev. Michael Terranova
WiseWoman Press
Vancouver, Washington, 2010

Lesson I

Missing

Mark 6:17-29 Jan 6, 1895

LESSON II

The Prince Of The World

Mark 6:30-44

Has anybody discovered the actual name of that something about himself that is adversary to everything he does and says? We have a Bible that calls it by a multitude of names as though hoping by some one of them to catch us every one.

"I am against thee," saith the Lord, *"Agree with thine adversary quickly," "He was moved with compassion."* In this last text the word "he" refers to that one who accompanies the artist while he is painting realism to delight an admiring and praiseful world. The artist hides it, stifles it, ignores it, but there it is. He paints the young deer's mute but hopeless appeal to the beautiful Duchess as her white fingers are pulling the trigger with straight aim between its eyes.

That "He," that is the compassionate one, stands close by the beautiful Duchess, while her cold but wonderful eyes measure distance and poise, "He" stands close by every man of empire and republic, Prince of India, or banker of America, an eternal companion. "He" cannot be shaken away, laughed away, danced away, shot away, "He" is the compassionate one. Did you ever notice that "He" while you stood before a great artist's amusing description of some little terrified animal being teased by dogs and laughing children?

That "He" is the same as the "adversary." It is the same as the "Lord." The New Testament sometimes calls it "the lamb that was slain." It now and then calls it "the lion." It has even spoken of it as "the poor." The New Testament is all given over to showing how you would act if you took notice of that one who is eternally keeping you company, but hates every movement you make, *"Behold, I hate your feasts and despise your feasts*, saith the Lord." Here you will see that it is called a "hater."

The Old Testament is given over to promising that one man shall appear some day upon earth who will watch the "hater" that keeps him close company so steadfastly that he will be the compassionate one. For it is shown that to be absolutely opposed to the government of this world is to be the supreme hater. The supreme hater of the prince of this world is the compassionate one.

The prince of this world ordains that "life evermore is fed by death." The compassionate one abolisheth death. The prince of this world saith that if I hurt a fly I am a coward, but if I kill a thousand oxen per minute I shall be highly honored as a noble soul. But the Old Testament promised that one man should stand up boldly and so defy that principle that he should change a world's liking for it till it should come to pass that "he that slayeth an ox shall be as though he had slain a man."

The New Testament declares that the compassionate one is that everlasting comrade of all men, as allies, who sometimes whispers to them, "How would you like to be in that helpless thing's place?" The New Testament goes so far as to say that this object lesson of slaying and slaying which the prince of this world sets up shall disappear with its captivating assurances that it is the living God who paints the soils and ethers with "survival of the fittest." He leadeth captivity captive."

The man who knows how to delude me into turning away from my "adversary" knoweth how to shut up my mouth so that I cannot plead well for earth's victims. But the Old Testament promiseth that somewhere about this year of our Lord, 1895, one "shall lift up his voice for the dumb in the cause of such as are appointed to destruction." No splendid artist can hush him up. No billions of money can buy him. No leading magazine can scorn down his influence, "For before the day was I am He, and there is none that can deliver out of my hand."

The New Testament tells of some brilliant Christian ministers who were so mighty in word and work that the very demons disappeared where they went, who wanted compassion and comfort for themselves on the desert march of earth, but who wanted the unfed multitudes driven away from compassion and comfort. (Mark 6:30-44) A young carpenter who had given the attention of his life to that "hater" accompanying him, and had become so one with it that he was as compassionate for beggars as for Christian ministers, insisted on all the multitude being as well fed as the Christian ministers. This astonished them so that one of them said sarcastically: "Would you have me give up my salary for these cattle?"

The Preaching Of Paul

The young man who had become all compassion ignored the question. In our day we say: "My good sir, if I should give to every man and woman that asked of me I should be a beggar myself." The young carpenter who had watched the unfailing "hater" within himself answers with one answer. He ignores the danger of "my being a beggar" by giving; "Give to him that asketh thee, and from him that would borrow of thee, turn not thou away."

This young man had watched that terrible comrade, of the Duchess and the artist, of you and of me, world without end, until he had compassion — had compassion — had compassion — on the poor, the very poor; on the helpless, the very helpless. He touched even the low caste lepers with tenderness.

It is no wonder that Paul said he was thankful he had only baptized two people, for the baptized ones were getting so factional that they boasted of being of John, of Cephas, of Christ. He wanted it distinctly understood that he brought no new religious system to hypnotize people into following him with, and that there was but one thing he kept his eye on, and that was his soul, his own soul, which he had hidden and choked and ignored and crucified by persecuting people, in spite of its following him up, till one day it had taken him utterly in hand, and he called it Jesus Christ. So he preached Jesus Christ; not religion, not science, ." . . but he that liveth in me. He that ever liveth to make intercession."

Today's lesson tells us how we act when we have watched that terrible something that goes around with us protesting against a certain class of men taking possession of the green earth's fields and crowding another class out of possession because they seem to be small witted and limp-muscled. This lesson shows that there cometh a day when we say: "Have thine own way with me!" And it tells how the granaries may groan with plenty and the coal mines with coal, under the lock and key of such as pay the artist for amusing them with praise of the lamb, but the one who is all compassion will rise up and show the defeated how God can feed them.

The Object Lesson Of The Young Carpenter

This lesson makes an object lesson of a young carpenter who had kept watching his own soul for over thirty years, when he found that one name of his own soul was "Heavenly Father." He found that he could do nothing working at carpentering and saving his wages that would pacify that strange comrade that followed him, and all other men also, forever and forever, so he left off manual labor and went to thinking. He thought and thought and thought till he was as adept as a modern rishi in hurling thoughts around which could captivate other men's minds and cause them to fall down and obey his orders. But he found that sending good thoughts around and abroad was not any more pacifying to that strange everlasting soul of his than manual labor.

He discovered that one might just as well go missioning with tracts and school books, a dying savior and opium, as to be hurling thoughts through the airs to govern his heathen neighbors with. So he left off thinking and told the terrible one to have its own way with him. At this point he called it "Heavenly Father." *"Take no thought for your life what ye shall eat or what ye shall drink; nor yet for your body what ye shall put on — for your heavenly Father knoweth."*

He found that this same comrade of all men alike can actually take us all up and let us down, clothe, feed, comfort us, whether we have been good prayerful people or bandits, and that without our doing anything for it or even thinking anything about it, if we will only turn and say unto it. "Have thine own way with me." It remembereth not one second the bandit's conduct. It remembereth not one second the minister's prayers. They are nothing to it. All is nothing to it. Itself is all that it knows.

He found at one point that it can empower the lips of a man so that nations will tremble at its utterances, even if he is only a slave in an island and has never read a book, if he will only watch the ever accompanying something in him which sometimes acts as protest, sometimes acts as hater, sometimes acts as compassionate one, and say unto it, *"Have thine own way with me."*

Keeping Count Of The Sparrows

He found at one point of eyeing it that there was no law of nature it was bound to obey, or no law of nature man or beast was bound to obey if the soul was their governor. The laws of nature are reverse to it. Shadows thrown down, casting opposite principles to its ways. Laws of nature run the cat after the mouse and the duchess after the deer, but its laws annul nature at every turn, calling it "prince of this world," but nothing but sham from beginning to end.

The one who stands by the great magnate of our republic while he is "bagging birds" takes note of the birds as well as the magnate. Not a sparrow falleth without the notice of that one; which, means, that the magnate's soul standeth by and never gives him peace. The soul is always in heaven. Who could suppose that they torment little birds in heaven? The soul is called "The Father" because it was the starting point of all men alike.

Whosoever watcheth his mighty soul can say to the bird while the jaws of the cat are open to receive it "Flee, bird, with your wings, into peace." And to the cat, "You are fed," (Luke 1:53) and the heavenly way of living travels over the highway from the soul in heaven to the creatures that crawl and fly, and there is no more pain, neither sorrow nor crying.

It was at this point that the young carpenter of Nazareth felt the airs from paradise blow sweet over hill and mountain, and lifting his hands upward he looked into heaven, for the sake of the world, and showed all men how to be fed without looking any more to man, either to his factories or his religions. (Mark 6:41).

> "Oh, airs from the hills of glory blow;
>   Oh, life from the swells of the infinite flow;
> Thy light, my Father, it falleth on me;
>   Thy goodness, my Father, its manna is free."

The Arithmetic Of Earth And Heaven

At this point the young carpenter of Nazareth took the arithmetic of earth and lighted it with the arithmetic of heaven. Did five loaves of wheat and two fishes dare hint at incompetency to feed 5,000 men besides women and children? Did nature's law, that sham opposite to heaven's everlasting security, dare lisp that more timid fathers should toil in the field and thousands more swimming things should flinch, before enough food could fall to the welfare of his congregation? How silent nature was while the soul of a peasant held away on the deserts of Bethsaida!

No wonder that time is not reckoned forward from great Caesar's birth, nor from conquering Pompey's, but from the birthday of the Galilee fishermen's King.

Daniel prophesied that such would be the final effect of this wonderful boy's acquiescence with his own soul, that after some years one Michael should stand up in his name and show it as the right name for every man's own soul, and that one day it should spring on the world as an upsetter of all nature's laws in its conquering compassionateness for the hordes of witless, cheap beings challenged with offers of new military forces instead of with offers of food in Christian nations.

"The thrones of earth's kings shall be shattered
   And the prisoner and serf shall go free,
I will harvest from seed that I scattered
   On the borders of blue Galilee;
For I come not alone and a stranger.
   Lo! my reapers will sing through the night,
Till the star that stood over the manger
   Shall cover the world with Its light."

Oh! great for our world is that day when a man has seen his own soul's **majesty**! For nothing can stay its conquering arm when it hath been watched till it hath risen as compassion. While it standeth by as an adversary it moveth not. While it standeth by as a protest it speaketh not. While it is being struck and cut and slain as a sheep before its shearers **it** is dumb, so it defendeth not itself; but when it striketh as the hitherto untouched, and hitherto mute chords of compassion, the mountains flee away, the old earth rocketh as a billow, the Messiah in his glory steppeth forth from the beggars, the true God is visible.

Inter Ocean Newspaper January 13, 1895

LESSON III

Comments and Explanations on The Golden Text

John 6:25-35

Capernaum has two meanings, "the field of repentance" and "the city of comfort." The mystic doctrine of Jesus was repentance. His whole mission was to establish heavenly principles on earth. He Himself had practiced repentance till he had discovered exactly how to "bring forth works meet for repentance." It is generally supposed that repenting has reference to each one of us willfully forcing ourselves to leave off some petty fault or cruel practice. Closer investigation of the character of Jesus discloses the fact that to practice what he meant by repentance is to find the petty fault and the cruel temper quite fallen off from us and we have not used any will about it.

My manner of conduct is called my life. I am taught by Jesus that this conduct is sure to be beautifully exact after I have found out what He meant by repentance. The act of repentance is simply turning to look at my own soul. This soul I must call by name. The powerful transfixing, uplifting the name of my soul is strangely enough — not spirit, not God, not mind, — but the name of a character.

This soul of mine is always alive. It never dies. To take much notice of it is to manifest a good deportment in life. No matter who says I am mistaken, that soul will reassert often to me, "Because I live ye shall live also," and I shall go boldly on, knowing that I am right.

This soul was what Leonardo da Vinci was watching when he sat so many days before an altar cloth, and saw nothing at all outside of and before him. He was repenting. That is, he was looking at his soul that stood behind him. When his faculties all-together once touched the soul of himself they brought forth a work meet for such repentance. The altar cloth was a wonderful, wonderful work. It did not take him many minutes to paint it. It required no terrible exertion, toil, labor, will.

Every picture of Beethoven shows him seeing nothing forward from himself. His eyes are looking backward toward "him that sitteth on the throne." This was his practice of repenting. So transfixed were all his faculties by the enchaining splendor of his own soul that he brought forth works meet for a marvelous repentance. Listen to the strains of his matchless music. They are so alive with the soul's deathless tones, that though ages shall come and go, dynasties rise, and vanish, the sounds of his chords on the ears of coming man shall still wake memories of his first home in the bosom of God.

Why Mankind Loves Repentance

All men love repentance. They are in love with their own soul when they once catch sight of it. What shall it profit a man if he gain a million dollars per year and lose sight of his own soul? For the dollars go not with him forever bearing him on their wings of safety, but the soul goeth with him forever willingly bearing him on wings of glory into happy realms where death and disappointment never yet entered.

Jesus, son of Mary, repented for the purpose of bringing forth another kind of work than painting or music. He looked backwards "to him that sitteth on the throne," and found that all heaven was his own to do with as he pleased. He said; "*I will have heaven on earth.*" It was a stupendous request. The arches of heaven rang. Glorious beings sped from star to star of the night skies of such a realm as no man's eye hath seen, to tell how "beyond man's demands as hitherto recorded was the call of the peasant of Galilee, *Thy kingdom come on earth.*"

With his eye fixed on his own soul Leonardo da Vinci took no note of the cold or the heat. Hunger and nakedness were not felt; they could not have been felt. Suppose a jeering crowd had called him a hypocrite and a knave, think you he would have cared? Day after day he sat watching. So Jesus, man among men, with his eyes set toward heaven, let his contemporaries call him a glutton and a winebibber, let his neighbors spit in his face, let them nail him to a cross, let them shut him into a tomb, but he never once took his eyes from their watch into heaven. Day after day hath passed by. His very teachings have been twisted into excuses for making hardship and poverty and despair for earth's children; but still, with his unyielded demand, his face is still turned toward heaven for a new set of principles to reign on earth.

Does anybody see any signs of the swift strokes of some supernal artist on the canvas of time? Doth any ear hear the coming of the hosts of heaven over the triumphant vision of Jesus the watcher?

As the altar cloth felt the thrilling touches of a soul-skilled hand and trembled at the swiftness of its movement, so Jesus Christ said that the instant he should touch the kingdom with all his being, he would return with his work meet for the repentance he had elected. His coming should be quick as the lightning that springeth from the East unto the West.

Explanation Of The Day's Lesson

No matter how the nations should be acting; no matter how the mind of man should be capering among fantastic religions which had no power in them to turn a man's eyes to repenting; no matter how long the time might have seemed, when his coming should begin it would be instantaneous.

"The Lord whom ye seek shall suddenly come."

Today's lesson explains that the man who is still asking of his own soul in its kingdom for one marvelous piece of work called transformation of earth into heaven, while he was visible to man, before they erased his form, used to work miracles. He would have stayed among them working miracles, but they spat upon him and buried him. Do not imagine that he minded little items like death and burial while his eyes were set into the kingdom with a purpose more stupendous than Beethoven's. He took the shame easily. It was nothing. A larger ministry than safety for himself was on his heart. The eternal security of all men was his quest.

And when they had found him on the other side of the sea they said unto him, *"Rabbi, when camest thou hither? —* (John 6:25-35) He had walked across Galilee into Capernaum, but he did not tell them of it. They had perceived that he went not in the boat with Peter, James, John, Stephen, Matthew and the rest of the Christian ministers, who had taken the usual conveyances of man across sea, while he had lifted himself by the mystic power of looking backward.

To this day, it is still a powerful thing to do. Look back and try it. It will stop your mental processes so that you do not come at knowledge by reasoning out logically from given premises. You get it by inspiration. This is walking across on a ray from heaven, instead of rowing across in a boat with oars.

It will stop your manual performances so that you do not do anything you might naturally be expected to do, yet you turn out ten times the work expected, and arrive at the goal where you were wanted before the best toilers among them. This is by inspiration. No inspiration ever came to any man except he were repenting. That is, had his eyes on something behind him, that by seeing forward, he must dig and row, connive and contrive, compete and jump, in order to approximate unto.

The act of walking across a turbulent sea was one of the powers conferred by repentance. It was a great thing to those who were working out their life by progression forward. So they said; "What shall we do that we might work the works of God?" He who was watching his own soul was so absorbed in it that he was it. Being his own soul, he was their soul also; for soul is one. So he answered; "<u>Believe in your comrade.</u>" He knew that their soul was their comrade, as my soul is mine, and yours is yours, forever.

Last Sunday's lesson was a very bold one. It proclaimed that even the Duchess who is shooting deer has a fine needle lancing its way through her being that will show up all shining in unbreakable majesty one of these days, instead of being covered by ambition to be praised as a good shot. If she lives to be 90 years old she can't get rid of thatneedle. Its name is compassion. The best way to do with that needle is to say to it! "Have thine own way with me." This will stop that ambition to be praised for skilled cruelty. But she will not lose her desired need of praise. She will cut across the seas of mortal ways by a wonderful inspiration that will be just as satisfying as the Queen's medal of honor for slaying an unprecedented number of pleading dumb things.

"It may not be my way,
  It may not be thy way,
And yet in his own way
Our God will provide."

For that fine needle of compassion which pompous men and women cover up under their cloaks is really their God. Its other name is soul. Its conquering name is Jesus Christ. Its ethical name is compassion. It will provide the Duchess with praise if she has her heart set on praise, even as it provided da Vinci with a design and Beethoven with a sonata.

But not by eyes gazing outward, forward. "They shall go no more out forever." It is by eyesight turned backward. This is miracle working always and forever for anybody who tries it. Last Sunday's lesson called all this outward world's transactions, deflected shadows of the kingdom behind us — close behind us; nigh at hand.

Man Forever Seeking Shadows

It defined all appearances as images in a mirror. Turn backward from the images, and there are the realities. This is the way all original, masterful, noble minds do. By a sudden prompting they reverse their vision. Then they paint objects with their new vision. So beautifully do they paint that other people gaze and adore.

Plato quoted from an old figure of man's estate by describing man as forever looking at shadows on a wall, instead of turning around to see true things. By looking back with the eyes closed all the healing miracles have been wrought.

Some people have spent their time making addresses to their God, memorizing and repeating formulas of praise. This has helped them to keep their vision fixed.

Today's lesson has for its main point the short turns that may be made in every department of human need. Over again it insists that the soul, which follows a man everywhere, has ways of fulfilling all the needs of each man's days utterly different from any that we now use.

At Capernaum with its double meaning we get a double lesson. First, repent; second, comfort.

Repentance is not first and primarily leaving off sinful actions. These leave themselves off. Most of the highly praised principles of human conduct and most of the descriptions of our God are as sinful as murder. Take this poetry as an example of pure sin:

*"Heaven wants fresh souls —
   Not lean and shriveled ones;
It wants fresh souls, my brother —
   give it thine."*

The soul is already in heaven, where there is no shriveledness imagined against even the most unhappy of us. Swedenborg said that the angels never could see any of us but as wonderful beings. The leanest and most wretched among us is accompanied by a shining soul. If we look at the soul when it pinches us with an inward protest we have repented. To say to that inward protest which we feel against our lot; "Have thine own way with me" is repentance. We do not then remember how it feels to find faults in our family. We have repented. All mankind are in love with the repentance practiced by Jesus Christ. Conduct, deportment, had nothing to do with his meaning. Did Leonardo da Vinci have to lash and pound his deportment? Was it not taking care of itself?

A short cut to all manner of new ways of doing great things is by today's lesson illustrated to follow the watch of the compassionate stir in man. You often feel sorry for a helpless creature.

The City Of Repentance-The City Of Comfort

That is compassion. It is the soul. It is the Jesus Christ in you. Say unto it: "Have thine own way with me." Soon it will take you into a new state of affairs by a short route. It doesn't take all day for the Jesus Christ in you to operate when you give it your attention.

It is the true God. It does not depend upon the opening of the car shops to provide for you and your family. It does not depend upon good sales of real estate or sugar-cured hams to feed you and your family. It would be a good plan for all who have been supposing that protection, security, home, plenty were dependent upon material business to practice noticing the lance of the soul in them as companion, and telling it to have its own way over all this earth.

For immediately it saith: *"He that cometh to me shall never hunger."* (Verse 35)

Immediately it would take us from memorizing what our ancestors had found out about, snails and suns, wheels and religion, for we should see that it had all counted for nothing — nothing. Death and poverty were still flaunting victorious flags before those good scholars. (John 6: 58)

Immediately it would take us from practicing prudent sight in calculating on how to maneuver with men, affairs, wheels, politics, money. Those who had tried all the foresighted speculations of the year 1 were nonplussed at the failures and want that faced them. (John 6:34)

This lesson is the "rest" lesson, "They rest from their labors, and their works do follow them." What a rest for man to cease from judging by past experience. What a rest for man to cease calculating for a future!

Have we not always been told that repentance was salvation? "In returning and rest shall ye be saved." The city of repentance is the city of comfort. "The Lord will comfort his people." Repentance is gazing backward at the soul. That which follows repentance is rest. That which follows rest is works. Yet not I do the works; but they follow. So hath the Lord comforted Jerusalem.

Inspiration At The Gate Of Every Man

It is true that the short cuts are nigh the compassionate. For it is easiest for them to say, "Have thine own way."

And it is true that sudden inspirations are nigh, even at the gates, of any man who hath caught himself facing up the indisputable evidence of this day's situation, that his forefathers did not tell him right, his pulpits are as dependent upon outward movements as his manufacturers, but Jesus Christ taught that to live securely we must surely draw straight from heaven. (Verse 33)

Whosoever calls this manner of interpretation too idealistic to be practiced let him take notice of the deep wish within his heart that it were true and practical. That deep wish is the stir of his soul. We have been having lessons which showed that all stir of inward protest is call of the soul for man to turn unto it and offer it its own way with him. Today's lesson is just as emphatic in showing that every time a wish moves within us it is again, in another fashion, the same soul call for us to offer, in our own language, all that we are to the management of that divine mover. (Verse 30) Lean hard on your wish. It is alive. Lean steadily to it. (Verse 29)

Peter had just been trying to walk the waves with Jesus, but he had taken his mind's eye off the transcendental principle of sustainment from heaven, and looked down at the ordinary experiences of mankind. He had begun to sink into the waters. Of course he would sink watching this human sea of turbid beliefs in ways contrary to the soul's ways without a boat and oars. He must not set his watch that way if he wants safe transit.

To whoever watches his wish watcheth the Jesus Christ in him. The waves of misfortune drown him not because his eye is on his own wish. The billows of death roll close to his feet, but he lives, for his eye is on the upbearing one. The age of failure and fear swells under his pathway, but he is as fearless of evil as Jesus on Galilee.

The instant a man begins to fear that the Jesus Christ principles are not practical in this world of neck to neck and sword to sword he feels the billows cold at his feet. He still has one helper near. It is his deep wish that they were omnipotent here on this earth. That deep wish is the touch of Jesus Christ on his face, to call him to lean hard. What a name for so many movements! The absolute and eternal fact is all enshrined within one name.

> *"Ridge of the mountain wave, lower, thy crest!*
>   *Wail of Euroclydon, be thou at rest!*
> *Sorrow can never be, darkness must fly,*
>   *Where speaks the light of light, Peace, it is I!"*

Inter-Ocean Newspaper January 20, 1895

LESSON IV

Comments and Explanations on The Golden Text

Matthew 16:13-25

These International Bible Lessons have sufficiently identified themselves with each man's experience so that whoever keeps watch of them may read the signs of his own lot. Today's lesson refers to the opposition which people meet in the very communities and families where they merit the most cooperation.

According to the lesson on Joseph, which was devoted to the metaphysical plane, with its illustrations, the mind of man is toned up by hatred and cursings as the physical body is invigorated by strychnine and arsenic.

Joseph never amounted to anything while he was staying at home preaching about the sun and moon as so and so, about the prognostics of corn sheafs, etc. But when the people he adored and daily served set to criticizing him causelessly, the very stones of Gilead rose up and turned into camels, bearing spicery and balm to seat him in due season on the throne of Egypt.

If you are an Aristides at the date while you are reading this lesson the people whom you have most ardently served are finding most fault with you. They banished Aristides for being too just. If you are a house servant somebody is complaining. If you are a minister of the gospel the strychnine of criticism is being administered. This is most excellent January tonic. Now is your time to take account of stock. What principles are you managing your life by? How have they worked thus far? (Matt 16:13-23)

The story of Abraham is a correct illustration of how a man would eventuate who should turn to that streak in himself which is his native-born faith in a divine being. Every child has a streak of native confidence or faith in a surrounding power.

When Abraham digged a well his neighbors got to conniving to appropriate the well. So he rose up and departed and digged another well. He repeated this process of digging new wells when oppositions met him because his streak of confidence was independent. One spot was as diggable as another for him. His sympathy for those who could not dig their own wells was prodigious. This faith streak should be pointed out to all young people, for it is the surefootedness of any life that knows how to watch it scientifically.

Right Of Ajax To Defy The Gods

The lesson of Jacob was an illustration of how any child would turn out who would discover that he has a streak about himself which is never defeated. Every child should be told to watch that undefeatable something within himself.

The young Ajax shook his clenched fists at the gods adored by his parents and swore to succeed in spite of them. That was right. If there was any clause in his horoscope which read that the gods were opposed to his success, he was self empowered to defy them. For the success streak is equally donated to every young one, whether its name be O'Flarrity or Victoria. Let him once turn it loose on this Globe and no god can withstand him. Even a syndicate would dissolve for a child who should secretly give his Jacob streak free rein.

The story of Beethoven is a story of modern life and times, but it is just as illustrative of the effect of focused attention to one inborn trait. Lofty sentiments conduce to nourishing native chords. If a child has a love of music and keeps his mind or his gazing faculties on that love he will find all this world rising up and moving toward him with offers of help to make that which he watches prominent. If he catches sight of some lofty principle his musical genius will have divine nourishment as well as personal friendships. Of course Beethoven had Count

Kinsky, Prince Lichnowsky, and others to patronize and befriend him as a legal tribute to his concentrated gaze on his inward love of music, but there was one mighty sentiment he nourished himself, with which he made the sun shine on his genius to draw it forth and up into strength and beauty.

Get at the secrets of all notable geniuses, and you will find such nourishing sentiments as fitly correspond with the style of friends and the style of opportunities that follow them up.

Beethoven copied some lines found by Figeac on an Egyptian temple, and kept them under a glass on his private desk where he could read them often. They read as follows:

> *I am that which is,*
>   *I am all that is, that has been, and shall be,*
> *No mortal hand has lifted my veil.*
>   *He is by himself, and it is to him that everything owes existence.*
>   *He Contrived The Quarrel Of Cain And Abel*

These lines nourished his musical genius. If given to a child whose mind was gazing at his one undefeatable chord, that child would find his native powerfulness stimulated to noble achievements by them. This lesson is all peculiarly adapted to the very young among us. That does not hinder the wrinkled and gray-headed from rising up and doing likewise, but generally they are so engaged in speculations of how they can keep their salaries or invest their wealth that they give merely a passing nod of approval at the saving principles, or maybe suggest or combine against them as undermining to orthodoxy.

Today's lesson finds the man — set up by Matthew, Luke, etc., to illustrate how a child would act who had watched for thirty-two and one-half years the shining, unearthly, independent something in himself, which hath never yet had any name — hurrying away from Galilee on account of so much opposition to himself. He could have used his genius to defeat all his opponents; he could have been made king of synagogue orators and king of Jew religionists and Greek scholasticism, but he was pledged to matching the shining, unnamed splendor, which he discovered in himself, and pledged to letting it be himself. To take a competitive place among the secular rulers of his day would have been no demonstration to himself or anybody else of how that interior illumination would act when told to have its own way.

To compete with Jay Gould on his own lines of enterprise and defeat him would be the same miserable old quarrel of Cain and Abel continued. The man of Nazareth was not here to fight me on my own ground; he was here to show me the glorious possibilities open to me on his ground. Thus he remained not among the people whom he had been serving with his life-blood, not a moment when they wished him to depart out of their coasts.

Influence Of Great Names On Character

This lesson is to proclaim to all people who are under the hail of criticism, whether the typesetter or the pulpit mogul, to give a name to the undefeatable streak in themselves. Christian Science brought out the much- covered principle of naming.

In a high or low grade we always see every quality we name. We always experience more or less the character of every man or woman whose name we speak or think. The way we speak or think corresponds to our grade. A serf of Russia would get a different grade of experience from repeating the name Demosthenes from what an American schoolboy would get, but both of them would feel more eloquence of tongue stirring them.

A certain New York lawyer who studies Shakespeare often feels the same quality of fire in his brain and heart that he is confident the Avon wonder was kindled with.

The young man called Jesus had been watching the movings of divinity within himself from the day he first heard how King David had declared that all the help he had was in himself and had named that inward help "Lord." He had stood in the midst of his neighbors, and, by keeping all his eyesight on his inward Lord over matter, had turned water into wine.

Every child has an inward lord over matter native to himself. Our schools do not tell him that his inward lord over matter does not demand of him that he pound and melt and trade in matter to govern it, but Jesus taught this fact.

Jesus had stood in the midst of a pathless desert and watched the streak of compassion in himself till it rose in the majesty of its everlasting nature and multiplied food for the multitudes. Our churches have not taught our butchers and our sweaters that the compassion streak born in them is more powerful than their ability to start out as poor boys and by skillful manipulations of half-witted swarms to pile up fortunes. But Jesus taught that fact. No Sunday school has ever proclaimed that each boy and girl would find the compassion streak in himself his public benefit potentiality. But Jesus taught it.

Protest Test Of Jesus

This same Jesus told the same multitudes whom he had fed that the absolute working factor in themselves was their inborn wish that God from heaven would do all things for all this world by some other way than the competitive, unreliable methods in vogue.

Seneca was very sly in his conduct. He told his audiences they must not look for any powers, or privileges, or demonstrations, or rewards, or anything whatsoever, but they must adore abstractions. The obedient crowds tried to do as he said, and thus being off guard he got $15,000,000 away from them. He could not identify himself with all alike.

But this Jesus had leaned hard on his inner wish that mankind might have enough to eat, without having to depend on whether their neighbors ran their factories four hours per day or all day. It was his inner wish that those poor, tanned-up grandmothers should share and share alike with Seneca and Pompey. He leaned hard on his inner protest, against unequal distributions of goods, and against even the powers of nature as seemingly pitted against the feeble, till he became an absolute rebel, and that made him absolute God.

He was preaching the equality of the inner spirit, and was devoting his whole power, wisdom, money, time to the audience, when they got to criticizing and complaining so much, that he left them.

So here he is, the living evidence of how definite it makes any mind to swallow its natural dose of the strychnine of unmerited rebuke. Now is the time to name that noblest motive you know you have been working with by its final name. It is the name of everyman's kindest purpose. Speak it boldly. Here we are taught that it is not Abraham; it is not Joseph; it is not Beethoven. (Matt 16:14.)

The Proclamation: "We Look Ahead"

The tongue that tries to call my divine motive by the name John the Baptist is hushed up. (Verse. 14) My motive, if I have been leaning hard on my wish to do great kindnesses, is not a preacher of doing good by and by. A good wish has the salt of this minute in it. Peter says, "Now!"

It was speculative philosophy which spoke in Plato saying, "We look for one to come, who shall lord it over nature." Seekers after truth are John the Baptist. Philosophers are seekers after truth. This man Jesus never said he was seeking truth. He said, "I am the truth." He took some fishermen who could not write their names and told them of their own divinity so definitely that into the blank ethers of speculative philosophy, ages upon ages proclaiming, "We look ahead," those men set the glittering stone of "the Messiah has come."

So Peter, who had to employ an amanuensis (scribe), who was an impetuous liar, (all these by world estimates) through his bold ability to name the shining divinity in carpenter and fisherman has always been a synonym of authority.

The proudest cathedrals of this world rest on Peter the Rock. But their actual rock is their bold assumptions. The very name Peter carries power in naming destiny, so that, step by step, not Herod, not Pilate (those aristocratic families who never could have had Peter tramping over their lapis lazuli floors), but the cowardly liar of sacred writ, is the surest name to remember to startle native boldness up.

"Boldness hath genius, power and magic in it;
  What you can do, or dream you can, begin it!"
Knowledge Which Is The Living God

What is this motive that prompts us to do a kindness to our neighbor? The Peter of us answers this question promptly: "The living God."

What is that deep wish that stirs the hearts of men and women to say: "The good reigns now, no matter if evil looks powerful?" The wish itself is the living God. It is the Peter quality that boldly names it so. Only Peter would dare to call his wish his God.

What is that knowledge that rises up within you that you have done nobly, divinely, though you are a wanderer and an exile, like Abraham and Jesus, for your services, though your employers turn you adrift, though you feel the powder of unmerited rebukes? The knowledge itself is the living God.

The Peter churches are stupendous because they have kept to their inaugurated practice of boldly naming what they mean to see carried out, and by keeping that name going on the blank ethers, where no such thing is known, they finally make the name a fact.

The knowledge that you are right is the living God. Call it so. The knowledge that you have done the best you could is the living God. Call it so. The knowledge that you are not less nor more than any others, but are yourself as you are, is your living God; and even if you feel yourself defeated, call your knowledge that you have no right to be defeated. Yea, call that knowledge also the living God.

Let not your reckoning of your present status of misery name you as unequal to swallowing all the criticisms and complaints that fall to your lot. You know that all that comes to God in its primal fact is God.

Inter-Ocean Newspaper January 27, 1895

LESSON V

The Transfiguration

Luke 9:28-36

The object of today's lesson is "Karma and Escape," Luke 9:28-36. In symbolic classics it is Moses and the Lamb.

There is an unexplainable fact in the Universe. Though reason should fly and spread itself within you to the measure of seven Socrates and ten St. Pauls it would still find itself unable to account for this fact in the Universe. We have to use a department of our being quite different from reason to discover it. Its name is Escape.

If any one chooses to get accurate interpretations of Scripture stories let him denude his mind of what his school teachers taught him, for what they said, even in his Sunday School Class was hypnotic suggestion and nothing else. It has shrouded the limpid splendor of his native mind with some rags and tatters of lingo, which nothing but the rise of the unreasonable rebel in him can ever tear off.

Descartes practiced tearing off from his mind the learning his colleges had sewed him up in. At every leap of the purple essence of his own inward mind he made an independent proclamation. It was not an echo. Looking at the state of this world with the bleared vision of hypnotized subjects what do we see? We see the happy worm starting out for his breakfast and the robin darting after him and making mincemeat of him. This is the phenomenon. The opposite of it is Fact. We see the thinly clad youth holding out his ignored hand to the millionaire. This is phenomenon. The opposite of this is Fact.

Anybody who has so many mummy cloths of instruction on him that he sees how powerful are poverty and despair, is an abject slave to phenomenon. He must unwrap his soul of the suggestions it is covered by. Then he will see Fact. There is a way to unwrap the most mummified among us and to expose the shining essence of original knowledge identical in all.

The Survival Of The Fittest

That set of movements which we call "survival of the fittest," whereby the luck of one man is the failure of another, and the pleading terror of the stockyard cows is the banker's breakfast, — is Karma. It is accountable phenomenon. It is the mummy cloth of suggestion, winding its cycles and circles round and round, age in and age out, till somebody rebels because he has espial (noticed) the Fact.

Whoever watches phenomena, weighting and counting and hoarding matter, and calling what he has gathered up "learning," let him spend a few minutes each day unlearning about these opposites to the Fact and he will be on the road to the Jesus Christ in himself, which is the unhypnotized native knowledge. There he will find that everything that parades as nature, from the stars in their collisions to the quarrels of the snakes, is one straight, absolute opposite to reality.

All reason is mummy cloth. It is Karma. It is conduct and consequence. If Napoleon III causelessly destroys Maximillian, Napoleon must be destroyed likewise, if they walk by law. If you whip your horse in anger you are to be whipped in anger; even if the periphery of the circle of the time takes you into the astral regions and back onto this earth again, that whipping awaits you. If you have piled up millions once you must be unpiled once. If a child wails with hunger, it once caused some other child to wail with hunger. This is Karma. This is law. This is the round and round of cause and effect. This is the refined hypnotism of admirable order. It is Moses.

Under its science warfare continues ages on ages to revenge former warfare. Under its scholasticism children are praised for painting cats, and there are schools for the same. Men are praised for inventing guns, and there are schools for the same; women are praised for cooking lamb, and there are schools for the same. People rise up from boyhood to maturity, drop their teeth and their wits at the same dates, cycle on and cycle off.

Absolute Escape From Karma

But this is not what Jesus Christ is in the Universe which is absolute escape from such orderly fol-de-rol. Under the reign of law I can never expect to escape the consequences of my remotest deeds. My lightest words bear accountability unbearable. If I say that I owe nobody and nothing I may find that my eyes appropriate that assertion, and when the sun shines on the faces of my children the eyes claim that they owe them no sight.

The fear of debt and the terrible struggle to keep from having debts to pay might settle into my ears and they would seal up with positiveness that they owed no hearing to sound. The complications of Karma are endless. Whoever puts his attention into cause and effect is soon bound to its wheel.

But the Jesus Christ in this universe is not involved in words which are bound to make results any more than it is involved in the drowning law of water. There is no cause for the Escape-free-cause. There is no accounting for that limpid glory called divinity wrapped within the organ grinder any more than there is any accounting for its lamb-like docility in being wrapped in the shrouding cloth of his seeming stupidity.

When John on Patmos saw the docility of the organ grinder's uncaused soul he called it the "lamb." He saw how the organ grinder might leave off noticing his shrouding environments and take to notice of his inborn divinity till he should suddenly find it bursting on the world in startling radiance. Taking notice of the divinity in himself is any man's transfiguration. The divinity within him can suddenly dissolve, with its unearthly fires, all the rags and tatters of his human lot.

Born in a manger, yet born with unspeakable glory under his swaddling bands, Jesus, the peasant, represented the cheapest of earth's children. Nurtured among the despised, yet nurturing transfiguring divinity, Jesus, the unkempt Nazarene, stood up for the tramps on a planet. Schooled in no university, yet acting in the name of the All-knowing One within himself, Jesus, the traveling man, took his time at overturning the school teachings of a globe.

The great Fact in this universe is the straight opposite of the seeming. — The straight opposite of law. — The straight opposite of everything in the unaccountable. Escape for all mankind from the dilemma of existence. It is unaccounted for in reason how Jesus Christ took death once for me and I may now go scot-free forever from death. It is the unaccountable Fact that Jesus Christ bore my sins and their consequence once for me and I may go scot-free from sin and its consequences.

Songs Of Karma And Escape

It is the unaccountable escape from consequences, which the live Fact makes for all the world. David had his eyes on that fact which is sure escape from cycles of law when, single-handed and unmailed, he displaced Goliath. It was not his own brave struggle; it was the easy victory of "him within him" that took bravery for him and he need not to be brave. That which takes and I go free is Escape.

There is the Song of Moses. That is conduct and consequence. That is Karma. There is the Song of the Lamb. That is escape from Karma. There is the law of the world, whereby the naming of a virtue salts me with that virtue; as, if I repeat the name God, I get domineering; if I repeat the name Om, I grow to be a sitting monument to nerveless peace. That is the Song of Moses. And there is the annulling of the law of the word, the escape from cause and effect, for which there is no law. This is the Song of the Lamb. "Behold the Lamb of God that taketh away the sins of the world."

Where did the song of conduct and consequence, cause and effect, get its scientific but half-fed announcements that there is no reality in pain, no reality in sickness, and no reality in cowardice? It got them from the Song of the Lamb that intones its eternal release through this universe.

The live Jesus Christ, Man in the universe, bore the pain of all men once, and they by looking at, beholding that fact, go scot-free of pain. The Jesus Christ took all the shame, disgrace, cowardice, and man by this unlawful song goes free, and thus is able to say, "There is no pain or cowardice for me."

He looks at the unaccountable and then can explain the accountable. He looks at what has been done and realizes his escape. The Transfiguration brought up today for our study was the effect of the Man's beholding his all-powerful nativity of divinity till it burst forth. This is the sure law of watching.

But that which is watched has no law. It had no beginning. It has no end. It does not move. But as human body and human mind copy it they are one instant along their espial of the act of disappearance. Human body and human mind need not move out of their chair of place, but they will see their hunger borne once for them by their own transfiguring divinity, and they shall go scot-free from hunger. They shall see their own divinity bear away their ignorance for them and they go scot-free of ignorance.

The Battle Is The Lord's

Thus, if Jesus saw all human Karma wrapped on purpose around himself, for the sake of the world, and watched the unaccountable achievement of his own divinity once for all mankind, who shall object to one such exhibition of divinity. Who shall try to account for such a choosing? Who shall not gladly accept the fact that such an achievement has taken place?

"They sang as it were a new song," said John. But its newness is only its seeming newness. It has been the actual background of all religions through all time. *"The battle is the Lord's,"* said David. *"Stand still and see what the Lord will do for you,"* said Aaron's brother.

In a temple of Siam the text on the image of Buddha read: *"Buddha disseminates the law as bait. With the loop of devotion, never cast in vain, he brings living beings up like fishes, and bears them into true understanding."*

The understanding power of the divinity in man has nothing to do with understanding of conduct and it consequences, or Karma. In that very non-understanding of conduct is its powerfulness. Who shall save us from my sins save he that seeth no sin in me? If seeing is being, why should I not go round and round bearing endless burdens while I see burdens? And why should I not be free from burdens if I see that to which all burdens are nothing?

*"For what thou seest, man,
  that too become thou must."*

Why should I not escape by watching and escape, even if there is no reasoning out such an escape? Shall I not rejoice that there is something unreasonable, unknowable, since reasoning and knowledge at their best working on mind and matter, have no power in them forever and forever to get me out of material and mental consequences?

The only truth there is to know is that Reality of the universe, which is absolute, unaccountable escape from all consequences of any word or thought or action. Moses and Elias, from the regions of the unknown, John and Peter in the world like today, did homage to the supernal splendor of the Lamb into whose untried efficiency a representative for the human race was casting himself that whosoever would look his way might escape from Karma or the teeth of regulated human destiny.

Inter-Ocean Newspaper February 3, 1895

LESSON VI

Christ And The Children

Matthew 18:1-14

Voltaire declared that in the economy of the universe if there were no God for man it would be absolutely necessary to make one. And it is certain that man always takes the consequences of exactly the kind of God he sets up. David found that to the merciful, Deity will show himself merciful, and to the froward (perverse) he will be froward.

Any man can set up an ideal and describe it till he makes as many see it as he has vital force to hold out against. It takes a great deal of vital energy to set up a great Spirit in the heavens and praise him up for his beautiful goodness to this world. The man who sets up such a monument of praiseworthiness has to hold his own against a savage number of scorners. "For he can't be all-powerful," reasons a whole army, "if he is good, or if all-powerful he would not permit such goings on." "And if he is good," whines another multitude, "and not powerful, why he needs as much pity and commiseration as the rest of us."

Man can make up a science of molecules. If he will hold on hard enough he can finally convince a planetful that molecules are so essential to us that we would perish without them. A man can establish a system of breathing through first the right nostril and then through the left one, and so seize hold of our firm confidence that we would practice that breathing system whether or no and for dear life, verily believing that we could never really find the divine presence except we did as he directed.

Time Will Teach Anything

The length of time we would be obedient would depend upon his vital energy. The younger a man is when he sets up a religion or a science, other things being equal, the firmer his hold on people's confidence, the larger his congregation of battered wills. If he can show signs in heaven above and earth beneath, like healing the sick and denouncing public sinners, age does not disadvantage him.

The great difference in the various gods held up by our different church denominations and the disputes that arise even among individuals as to the substance and disposition of the deity, show that there is something a little off from fact or the subject even to this day.

Today's lesson opens with a statement that the very best instructed on the God question were quarreling about what God was and would do with them, exactly as we are now quarreling, as long ago as Anno Domini 20. Each preacher is certain that if his god is God he shall have a very high seat among the saved. This anticipation of a high seat among the saved has kept up the courage of many a half-fed and under-paid minister of the gospel. (Matt.18:1-14)

The brilliant difference between Jesus of Nazareth and all the religionists he met was that he did not manufacture a deity. He pointed the way to something that already was and would remain forever, not unkind when we use him for that purpose and not gentle when we use him for mercy. Jesus of Nazareth showed man how to look into a realm where there is no call for mercy and therefore there is no mercy needed; where there is no knowledge of salvation because nobody ever was lost.

The New System of Converting

He instituted a system of converting, or as the theologues explain the word used, Matt. 18:3: "Turning about so as to face in the other direction." He would himself turn straight about and absolutely not see any of the performances of the gods, high up in front of the faces of the world. He turned himself so as to face in the other direction from the operations of nature. When water said, "I drown," he turned straight about and faced in the opposite direction. This so astonished water that it has never been recovered to its previous pomposity. Even today it will admit that any man who turns straight away from its drowning nature will be free from it. Jesus of Nazareth taught that it was a manufactured deity who injected the drowning principle into water, and inserted the stupefying incense among poppy-heads.

Jesus of Nazareth placed man at the belt line with his visional faculty. Look outward over the belt line and witness the pictures made by imaginations. Plato had taught the same principle. David had taught the same principle. The outer world, from the trees that lean and whisper on the horizons to the pain in a man's head, is all unreality. It is nothing. Every movement made in the visible universe is but an inverted picture in a looking-glass. We shall continue to study and measure orbits of planets which never existed, and diseases which had no starting place and all history, till the day we are converted. (Verse 5)

When the Faculties Are Set Free

The instant we are converted we begin to be free from all the conditions of this outer world. This conversion is made by the visional faculty. We are all able to stand at the belt line and turn our visional faculty straight around. We direct the searchlight of our vision backward. This is being converted. Every man wants to be converted. Every one wants to see the other country which lies in the opposite direction from the one he has looked at since he first opened his natural eyes.

It is singular why our wonderful preachers and scholars have spent so much time describing what can be seen by observations of the rings of tree trunks and bird tracks on rocks, the natural depravity of human hearts and the right uses of gold, when the actual fact has always been that to convert the vision was to see into a wonderful realm of eternal substance and from steady sight of that realm instantaneous understanding of tree trunks and bird tracks, human hearts and prosperity would be granted. *"Seek ye first the kingdom of God and all these things shall be added unto you."*

To be converted is not to be turned straight around from wickedness any more than it is to be turned straight around from book-learning and money getting. Jesus met the twelve classes of human beings who walk over this globe with the straight direction to turn themselves outside in and look the other way from what they were looking . . . To manage their perceptions like reversible telescopes. This is not a hard thing to do. Whoever does it will find himself feeling less and less dependent upon outward conditions. He will find himself living more nearly from his own center of gravity. He will have better judgment than he had before. His vision will light itself at the same altar fire where Jesus lighted his. The outer world will feel his mastery of it.

Vanderbilt, Gould, Paganini, Raphael, all converted their sight focus enough to master whatever they liked to handle.

How Skeptics Were Rebuked

Judas, the intellect of man, asked Jesus if good reasoning would not finally furnish a logician a better seat in that realm where power first hailed from than blind faith like James. Thomas asked if a discreet conduct all the way over this earth would not give a man more power than such blundering assumptions as Peter was always making, even though some of his affirmations ran higher than pious reasoning could follow. Thus disputed, they were all in like manner with Calvinists and Theosophists unto this hour.

But Jesus called a little child and said that it was their eternal object lesson. Take notice how little it sees of what is going on around it. Why? Because its sight is in heaven beholding the face of the "I AM." It will not be till it fastens its eyes out-ward over the belt line into matter too steadfastly that it will need converting. — (Verse 10)

Whoever can keep his sight running backward till he also sees the "I Am" of his own throne will care as little for high seats and worldly recognitions as the infant in arms. Will he be powerful thereby? If he sees the Father Point in himself he will be powerful. If he keeps seeing it he will be all Father. — (Verse 11)

If he sees outwardly always, studies outwardly always, over the belt line always he teaches these children to look into the opposites of the realm where they tend to look. The child's vision should direct his, not his the child's, if he is making realities of nothingness. One way is misery. The other is ability to transform misery. Why is man gazing, into a looking glass of images and beholding outwardly? Because he once chose to behold the opposite of reality, and he can plainly see it in matter and its laws.

Matter Must Be Subjected

It will be a triumphant day for the first man who can see matter and its laws and still keep his memory of the real kingdom without laws from whence he first came out. It will be the last day of matter and its laws when man not only remembers that he came forth from a realm which has no laws, but can by a glance of his eye upon nature cause it to fall at his feet as Jesus could do. For though man can sail the seas he is servant of water, not master if he is passenger on the Elbe. Though man can enlarge his brain muscles sufficiently to crowd down ten thousand little children into dark mines and build a church with a higher steeple than Cologne he is not master of gold when his brains fall out.

But it is man's immortal privilege to sweep the planet with mastery at every turn, and nothing in it should dare answer back, "We have a law." Things should know no law save what man is unfailingly above. — (Verse 2)

This unfailing master is not found by observations of matter and circumventing its plot, but by observations of that inner kingdom called the kingdom of heaven, which every man has the power to sweep his vision into. This principle cannot be told too often. Jesus of Nazareth repeated it every day for three years.

The fourteen verses of this chapter have three interpretations. One is the plain outer or physical, which causes a great deal of discussion as to the age of the child Jesus selected and causes a great difference of opinion on the subject of Palestine types of infants. It also leads to fears that if we do not save people while they are children they may be lost forever. By this manner of interpretation we were finally caused to see that Jesus loved children. By it the old fashioned domination over children has gradually relaxed.

Lessons Seen in Nature

The second is the metaphysical significance of child, which is docility of mind; teachableness, openness.

The third is the absolute meaning of child, which is the unspeakable, unknowable wonder that abides in the universe everywhere. It is typified by young things springing into manifestation everywhere. The earth is crammed with things just born. The airs team with new faces, multitudes on multitudes, too tiny to be seen. The waters turn up young mouths with every sparkle, too many for Euclid to count.

Thus is the wonderful One in the universe. Everywhere young, everywhere unspeakably lovable, everywhere irresistibly omnipotent God. Who had seen the perpetual young one facing every atom of our being forever as the ever recurring face of the infinite God till Jesus, the matchless, looked into heaven and lit his eyesight at the feet of the Lamb of mystery?

Any interpretation less than this is a millstone to drag us into time and law. Have we not had enough of time and law?

The twelfth and thirteenth verses are one: "*If a man have a hundred sheep and one of them be gone astray . . . if so be that he find it, he rejoiceth more over that sheep than of the ninety and nine which went not astray.*" Outwardly we would make a great study of the sheep and shepherds of old times. And by that interpretation we might get more gentle with animals. Metaphysically, we would declare that we must take all our herd of thoughts and keep them so under our will that we would finally not think a single false note; and we must take that one trait of envy or resentment that we have in us and chase it around and treat it with religion or science or penance till envy is not envy anymore, but it is converted into its redeemed opposite trait of praise.

The Longing of the Soul

The third translation from the literal sense to the divine nature within us is wholly different from metaphysics or physics. By it we know that the ninety and nine sheep are our best truths. They are good enough, worthy enough, but there is one fact that is diviner than truth, and it is one sight of our own everlasting soul.

While we have science classifying and arranging truth from simple premise to giddy heights of assumption, there is yet something unnourished, unsatisfied within us, but when we lay our faces on the buoyant bosom of our own innermost, unperishable spirit, we are able to commune with the Lord over fires and floods and famines, friend to friend. We feel the garments of nature falling off; the power of things on earth to hurt dissolves. Friends and foes, death and life come not nigh. This is the hundredth most precious one. Though we should know all the splendid religions and scientific principles of this nineteenth century by rote, and could explain them with glittering forcefulness, if we know not how to convert our sight from witnessing the opposite of the Jesus Christ, in this Universe, to single-eyed vision of our own spirit, whose demonstrating name is Jesus Christ, we must travel on over the plains and seas of this world, restless always, seeking always, something we know not what.

Ninety and nine truths flourish well sheltered under the roof trees of school and church in this hour, but the hundredth most precious message of conversion from observations of earth to actual sight of heaven by recognition of the everlasting spirit of power and glory within, now is for the first time being noticed. And this indicates the closing pages of time and law. Regard neither the cold nor the heat, the pains nor the pleasures of mind or body. The spirit that now riseth within thee calleth thy name.

Inter-Ocean Newspaper February 10, 1895

LESSON VII

The Good Samaritan

Luke 10:25-37

One of the first lessons taught by operative metaphysics is that every object appearing before us is a plain figure of some hidden idea of our own. A wounded man represents some wounded sensibility within our own heart. To neglect the wounded man would prolong the unhealed heart wound. By today's lesson, (Luke 10:25-37), we find that certain human figurations of our secret states of mind are called "neighbors." It was Luke's wish to present before our plain sight the object lesson of one man who lived through the mad fever called human by taking a wonderful remedy. With this remedy for the dying fever and the crying fever, and the formulating fever, Luke's hero was able every instant to detect the proper spring to touch, or the proper episode to force, to keep his "neighbors" in the correct attitudes.

Luke was a physician, and every sentence of his book breathes healing influences. Today's section takes up the subject of the remedy for human existence. It touches us every one from circumference to center. From the outer ring, where we originate corners or manipulate Wall Street, or even wash dishes and print circulars, to the inner point, where we know nothing at all, this section mentions us.

The inner point, where we know nothing at all, is our God point. This is very exasperating to many of us every time it is mentioned. But the highest doctrine of escape from the human fever is the mention of One Supreme Presence too pure to behold iniquity. Hence Luke makes Jesus fabricate a man, a robbery, a wounded body, a hotel, a priest, a Levite, and a Samaritan. Does he see those fictitious images? No. What does he fabricate them for? As a cure for human environments as they exist in persons and countries.

Offer of Absolute Good

Jesus of Nazareth had tasted the absolute remedy for human existence. Having tasted it, he was all divine. He offers his remedy to other men, also, that they might be independent of thieves, wounds, priests, and Levites. He offered them all a taste of free entity. The offer holds good now. It was an eternal offer. First, be metaphysically informed that every human being is a walking projection of your own secret ideas; and second, get acquainted with that region in yourself which never knows anything that is going on. Its way of knowing is indescribable. Its language unspeakable.

Jesus was able to keep his whole being intelligently poised in that region while yet he fabricated situations and persons exactly as men are now ignorantly fabricating them. Every man who asked him a question needed cure of something. The lawyer mentioned in verse 25 needed cure. He occupied a high seat in national affairs, and imagined himself to be so capable that even when he asked questions the world would tremble. Fortunately for his world he asked his hardest questions of Jesus, the one man who represented his own interior remedy for conceit. So when we feel contemptuous of the people in this world, and imagine that we would have made a better lot of them, we show that we do not remember, or never did know, that every human body is a walking object lesson of our own style of mind. "The world is my mental picture," said Schopenhauer.

In order to have us cured of this forgetfulness or ignorance Luke makes the lawyer ask the absolutely free man to explain freedom. A free man drops a snowstorm of free principles on us while we are watching him. If he is bound in any way he drops that bondage on us. This shows plainly that Jesus is a good character to watch. He had wrenched utterly free from earth's thraldom.

The Great Test Question

He ever liveth now as utterly free. If you ask me where he is I make bold to answer that, as he got entirely free from place, he is everywhere. "Lo, I am with you alway, even unto the end of the world."

The lawyer tempted Jesus with a test question: "What shall I do to inherit eternal life?" He meant untrammeled, fearless existence. "What is the remedy for human environments? I hate the way things are running on." — (Verse 25)

The answer touched the absolute presence first and then ran down the scale to daily events. "Love" is attention. The first lesson of mysticism is: "Attention." No matter what kind of attention you are giving, whether willing or unwilling, it is love. For love is pleasant attention at one of its poles, arid unpleasant attention at another of its poles.

Attention to the most central presence everywhere among us is love of God. (Verse 27) A slight attention makes us the Andrew type of man. He was one who studied hypnotism and theosophical communications as being very beneficial to mankind. Absolute attention makes us Jesus, who, from a clear view of the actual, was able to label these things instantly as bondages.

A slight attention sometimes makes a Peter type. He was one who understood the power of naming things to unname them, to dissolve or to bind them. When people are naming disease to dissolve them, and naming healthy states to fasten them into shape, they are practicing Peterism. Absolute attention makes a Jesus man who from his clear view of the actual, knows that healing the sick and fastening good morals among our people are bondages also. They are only hanging up temporary images for us to look at a few days or years.

How to Draw on the Eternal

Is it not a bondage to be unnamed of our maladies by Peter, and fastened into soundness by him, even by his secret mind, if it is not a soundness that will endure eternally by reason of our knowing how to draw on the eternal remedy?

How to draw on the eternal is the tempting question. The lawyer was discontented with such a world full of limited people. The best of them could only get so far with anything. The first thing they all knew, the best powers they had gave out.

Probably that "lawyer," who was both a pulpit preacher and a statesman combined, had noticed that his most attractively successful colleagues had suddenly lost their luck. Their former charm of personal presence had fallen off, and they were now depending on their intellectual magnetisms, their brain strength, but he could see some of the most powerful of even these getting to be old bores, venerable prosers. He was perfectly terrified at this prospect for himself. He had heard of an eternal re-enforcement. He sought it of the right man.

Luke shows how the Jesus man, now present in the universe, may be an increasingly good re-enforcement on all planes if questioned and listened unto.

It was a very simple remedy, but Jesus of Nazareth himself had taken it, and it made him every whit whole forever. It consisted in attending to that mighty wonder at his own head center, that region of him which knew nothing at all. That origin of knowledge which was not knowledge. That which was before truth. That which has its absolute cure for human existence in its very difference from human existence.

As the sensorium in the head is the seat of sensation, but has in itself no sensation whatever, so that seat of all knowledge in the all-knowing Jesus was absolutely without knowledge.

This was his panacea for ignorance. This was his remedy for poverty. This was his cure for trouble. "If you do not believe me," he said, "test me." I will make the worst wounded among the financiering policies of individuals and governments to rise well men. I will be a working principle of cure for thievery and its consequences in men and nations, and yet I will not see one single case of misery. I will know it all as a delusion. I will stand where I am and move not, but if any man looks my way I will have such an effect on him that he will no longer be a priest or a Levite. He will be a good Samaritan. He cannot help it.

A priest is one who preaches that all men are children of God but practices treating rich men better than he treats poor men. A Levite is a man who talks of the equal rights of the people, who poses as a philanthropist, but who started as a poor young man and drew himself several millions out of the people by business methods recognized as legitimate by the world but as dangerous as murder to face the hour of death with. (Verses 51 and 32)

A Samaritan is one who, though taught by priests and associated with commercial methods, yet believes in the safety of hand to hand friendship with all men. He is not afraid of being impoverished by helping men who need immediate bread on the street corners. He does not fear that by present giving he might lose his reputation as a hospital founder later on.

Ego a Samaritan Maker

"The Samaritan is the man who has looked my way," saith the Jesus Christ presence in the universe. The whole world is now hearing of the divine ego in each man. This causes each man to look more or less at his own divinity. His own divine ego is a Samaritan maker. Though he were a magnate in a powerful place, the friend of plutocracy, and the foe of the people, as in verse 30 of this lesson, the most dangerous attention he could undertake to give toward re-enforcement of his softening brain and loss of personal strength would be to that one everlastingly sure healer that he himself carries around, namely, his own changeless ego. For it would make of him a Samaritan. The proudest preacher in our pulpits who could not now do other than act as the priest of this lesson would perforce, *nolen volens* (though unwilling) become a Samaritan if he should hear of and attend unto his own ego that knows nothing and moves not.

The most solidly fixed Gould type of man, whatever his position in the government of nations, had better not look even at the mention in print of the divine ego that sits on the throne of his own being, knowing nothing of material movements. For it is a healer of the Levite type and none can stop it. Thrones must totter, palaces must dissolve, flesh be forgotten, mind be gone, for the Samaritan type of man is now making haste toward the robber world.

The Resounding Message

A message is sounding from shore to shore in these days that one man is as much divine in his native power and wisdom as another. The story of the present Jesus Christ in his untouchable majesty, dwelling in serf and prince alike, does turn man to look at his own royal greatness, and this look is his remedy for poverty and oppression. The serf may see the irresistible healer of shame that sits as an eternal king in himself. The prince may see the healer of his failing wits and dying muscles at the fire point of his own being. But serf and prince alike can be no more priest or lawyer, for when the earthly houses of their divine ego are dissolved they will have only heavenly qualities left while yet here on this globe.

The world does not have to wait for death and resurrection to turn first into Samaritan and then into Jesus. The very teachings that are sounding like Gabriel's trump on the nations today are doing up priests and Levites in the fires of oblivion. The poor, by their cold hearthstones, are turning, to look at the majesty of Godhead within them that never knew aught of misery, and that look is their remedy for misery.

Remedy of Acceptance

The sick are looking straight toward the divine center within them which never knew aught of sickness, and that look is their cure. The scholars of the world, so dissatisfied with the hordes of ignorant ragamuffins blacking their tracks, are turning to note how at their divinest *locus standi* (place of standing) their wisdom consists in knowing nothing, and this is their remedy for conceit.

Thus by the simple remedy of acceptance on the part of each human being that at the rendezvous where he meets with himself he knows no defeat, and this is the swiftest plan of assistance that could be devised for him, every one shall escape from the snares of the fowlers, and my people shall all go free. (Verse 37)

Balaam struck and pounded his faithful beast, but it could only groan. His rightful business was with the wonderful presence that stood near the beast. So this lesson teaches one man and all men that there is no remedy for poverty and sickness, and no remedy for any world state in belaboring men or systems, or bodies or minds, but that they are obedient beasts to bear us into secure estates when we reckon with the wonderful presence that stands near them.

Ages on ages have passed with the Balaams forever pounding politics and medicines, striking corporations and Tammanies, only to see them appear in other more disagreeable forms. But as the simple remedy for misfortune in Balaam's cause was to reckon with the presence of the Lord and not with the beast, so our simple remedy for the fever of human existence is reckoning solely and only with the Lord standing by.

Inter-Ocean Newspaper February 17, 1895

LESSON VIII

Christ And The Man Born Blind

John 9:1-11

Attention is the one secret of success in all departments of science. Attention to stones makes a good lapidary, mineralogist, or geologist. Attention to mind makes a mind reader, psychologist, reasoner. There is one science that is the focus of all the science. It is not the science of stones though by knowing it we will know all about stones. It is not the science of mind, though by knowing it we will know all about mind.

Nettesheim declared that the mysterious science, which to know is to know all other sciences, has never been attended by but a mere handful of votaries in all history.

Even a slight and prejudiced attention to this one science makes a man invincible like itself. To what splendid heights of immunity from earthly and mental thraldoms might we not be taken if our attention were to be wholly given to the science of sciences!

A knowledge of this science is promised to transform every atom and molecule of the physical body from its habit of shriveling and dying into a glistening bloom of beauty, deathless and smiling. A knowledge of this science is promised to touch everything and hope and feeling of the mind with enchanting enlightenment, so that its habit of losing its wits and talking too much will fall from its shameful conduct of attention to bones, sticks, worms, guns.

The pivotal center of this science is the point to focus the attention to. This pivotal center is always present with every man, waking or sleeping. It does not ask his language. It does not ask his money. It does not demand good behavior. Queen Victoria rides in royal state with her molecules and wits all spoiling because of non-attention to that pivotal center that attends her, as indifferent to the value of the gifts she is trying to cajole it with as her carriage step.

"*Vainly we offer each ample oblation,*
Vainly with gifts would its favor secure."

Ignorance Which is Universal

The mendicant woman on Congress Street sits no more ignorant of the glory of her own central fire than the orator whose thunder draws the dollars like hailstones from his congregation. This is evidenced by the humiliating fact that his bones turn yellow and brittle exactly like hers, and his intellect maunders and pules3 in due season to notify the universe that they belong to the same family.

Yet while the stars wheel on their trackless courses and the sun draws the oak and the mustard seed from dark tombs to laughing blooms, there waits for the world of man to recognize a science to glorify him from marrow-bone to unspeakable wish, so that he shall no more falter into death or imbecility.

> *"My son, give me thine heart.*
>   *And thy sun shall go no more down forever.*
> *The beauty of the Lord thy God shall be upon thee.*
>   *Nor shalt sing a new song.*
> *And the light shall shine upon all thy ways."*

Note the patience of the waiting science. Note the ravishing splendor of its touches, of light on mind and heart. Eternity too short to speak its praise. "For the Lord is not slack concerning his promises, but is long-suffering toward us." The sun would wait in silent majesty a hundred years without burning up your window sill; but when you should focus its rays with a glass it would not only consume the window sill but your whole house, promptly. Far greater than we can ask or even think are the works of the sun of those skies that hang over us. Under the glass of our simple attention to it, lo! the elements of nature melt with fervent heat, mind springs to open wide as the gates of an eternal morning, and body lets fall the rays of human customs.

What has constituted greatness in men through the cycles of light and darkness, day and night?

<u>Light of the Everlasting Sun</u>

Attention, by conscious intent or unconscious bent, to the patient's light, whose wonderful likeness they came to bear in their faces.

The one man who was born a slave, deformed, sick, contemptible, caught in his youth one far-off glance at the everlasting sun shining at the pivotal center of his existence. It drew him with the hands of its celestial radiance into its own embrace in justness to the attention he gave. The blows of his master had no hurting power. The ignorance of his mind had no fooling energy.

"Here on the lap of our mother we rest;
  God is our home."

A child born blind caught one far-away gleam of that sun whose waiting fires shine on you and me, and over the seas of time and over the dusty days of darkness it streamed as memento of his attention, bringing in its smile a man all shining with healing glory. In a moment his eyes were opened. *"A man that is called*

Jesus, anointed mine eyes and I received sight."
— (John 9:1-11)

There is a memento of all the glimpses of all men through all time embodied in one. All look at the central fire through prehistoric ages that had for its memento life, was gathered into one man once. *"I am the life."* That man is not dead. To this day he says; "Go wash in the pool of Siloam." *"I am the light of the world."* "I want to see that light that has for its melting glory the opening of my mind gates wide as eternal morning, the fall of my human destiny, the springing forth of my being as it was in its native beauty before I saw earth."

This is what we are really saying every day. In the object lesson set before us by John in this ninth chapter, tenth verse, the people put the question on the purely manifest miracle of healing from congenital blindness. But in their hearts they wished for the light of the world.

Reaching Toward the Unknown

There was never a man living who did not wish to know that science which could fulfill the restless leaps of his heart. There was never a man living who did not wish that he might know somebody or something who could show him how to outwit and circumvent blindness. But only now and then one of the monotonous march of time has cast his eye in the direction from whence the sun shines with power enough in its focused rays to open his mind and body with fervent heat and set him free from their darkness.

One day of ignorance is a cataract on the mental eye. One glance toward the sure fact that there is something somewhere that could show us something worth seeing would act like a magnet to bring somebody to tell us some news about the pivotal center. That news would be the clay on our eyes. If we should go and attend to the science given us by him we should not be utterly determined on blindness. Attention to the science of turning away from things subject to change, decay, death, to something that is not subject to change, decay, death, is a burning glass under a wonderful sun.

Under the heat of our attention to our own attending soul the flesh nature is burned to death. The conditions that limit us are burned to death. The thoughts that we have been sheathed in are burned to death. We are no longer blind; we see. Thoughts make a man blind. Attention to the thinkless soul burns away our thoughts. *"Take no thought,"* said Jesus. He that is free from thoughts through attention to his thinkless soul is invincible mind. To look toward one whose attention to his own soul — the pivotal center to which men pay no heed — has burned away his thoughts, is to feel the healing fire of his invincible mind.

The Teachings of Jesus

"Did not our hearts burn within us while he talked to us by the way?"

It is as useless to try to defeat or decry one who has been watching his own soul till its heat has burned his thoughts to death as to defeat or decry the omnipotent God.

Nature may hold toward his gaze the dimming vision and closing ears of her law of time, but her attentions to that man are her own destruction. He is as fiery as the sun toward which his gaze is fixed.

Nature herself shall feel the lightning lance of the look of a man who has seen his own soul. There is no sheath she can throw around the sun of the everlasting God. There is no sheath she can throw around him. He has become manifestly what his attention has been given unto.

Shall heredity in the flesh offer me a law binding me to blindness of eyes if I have turned away from heredity, in the flesh to watch my underived soul? Shall I not work the works of him that sent me by lancing the law of nature with the fire of my soul caught sight? This was the absolute teaching and living testimony of Jesus of Nazareth. He did not spend any time attending to microbes and bacillae, to cataracts, and dissecting tables; he gave all his attention to the soul sun burning at the center of his being, around which he knew all men alike were revolving. "They do not manifest in sin where I am," he said, "They do not manifest in blindness where I am. They do not have a law of heredity in sin or disease to which they can point. The soul sun that shines has its focusing rays in me, and I undo the wrapping rags of race with the burning touches of my presence all alight with that to which I am attending."

Three Planes of Interpretation

This lesson has its three planes of interpretation upon which we may walk;

1. Material.
2. Metaphysical.
3. Absolute.

On the material plane we have a careful picture of the beggars who followed Jesus in Jerusalem, and also of the pool of Siloam. We are told to load our minds with historic data. Let us know whether the water of Siloam was clear or muddy. Let us know whether the blind man was a homeless beggar or had a home and plenty of fresh-water fish to eat.

On the metaphysical plane our teachers explain Siloam as meaning pure principle, pure idea. Beggars are shown to be our hungry, eager thoughts that are ranging and roaming among books and preachings to find some substantial teaching that they can brace up on. But on the absolute plane we have again the vicarious atonement of that man of Nazareth who stood as a representative of all the kinds of people that ever lived or ever can live, and for their sakes became the burning glass of absolute attention to the mystery of his own soul till its hot rays made him the sun of eternal glory, to burn away the sorrows and death of all time for all men who would look his way.

On the cross of shame he watched the sun soul of his own fire center, and I, if I watch him even there, may feel the shame of my unmanageable destiny melt into the glory of that in me which is master of the stars of destiny at their very worst.

> *"In the cross of Christ I glory.*
> *Towering o'er the wrecks of time.*
> *All the light of sacred story*
> *Gathers round its head sublime."*

He that stood watching the everlasting God while hate and shame and pain wrought havoc, and through such darkness glowed with unspeakable light on born and unborn man, proclaimed even at the moment of touching a shiftless beggar's Karma-crowded life that vicarious atonement which no pulpit hath ever shouted forth, which no metaphysician has expounded. (Verse 4)

Principle of Vicarious Suffering

There is a principle in this universe of which very little has ever been said. It is that of standing voluntarily for a people and taking unto yourself all their pains and misfortunes, and, by their acceptance of your offer, they may go free from pains and troubles. If they will not accept your offer to take their pains and troubles they may carry and worry as much as they please. You may take this position with the resoluteness of a strong will, or you may take it from sighting the sun-soul within yourself.

In verse four of this lesson we are offered the vicarious atonement for work. Once for all the whole work of this world was done for all men. Why do they hug the practice of waiting with anxious interest for a millionaire to open his factories that they may work for him? Once for all the bread and meat and wine were made for a world. Why are they fearful lest they come to want of bread and meat and wine?

This is the night that was promised to man wherein he could not work. And this is the night that was promised to man wherein whosoever should accept the royal offer of one man to assume the burden of our existence, to assume the making of our bread, to assume the managing of our affairs, should find that there was nothing left to be done. All is well done.

There has been a kind of instruction forcing itself on this world to cause it to refuse the vicarious principle at its crowning exhibition, while yet every particle of healing done in our midst has been in a small way vicarious.

Mystic Science of Divine Healing

Every man who cures his neighbor man takes the sickness into his own possession and drops it down and away after his own fashion of vicarious office. He is an illustration, on a small scale, of what has been done in a great way on a tremendous scale for the born and unborn millions of a globe. Whosoever accepts that his bread and bed have been made once and forever for him will find them everywhere waiting for him.

If his fortunes crash, the very rocks will rend on his pathway to disclose the priceless gems they never will reveal save to that one that hath seen the highway of divine love embodied voluntarily once, in such omnipotent strength that all the hardships of all men, born and unborn, were nothing — nothing — nothing.

"There is a path which no fowl knoweth, and which the vulture's eye hath not seen."

The intellect cannot compass the mystery of taking my hardships and your hardships, our offenses and their consequences, and leaving us as free as the light forever.

The sordid seeker after gold end books, and house and land, and fame and name cannot detect its possibility. He believes that human nature is human nature the world over.

But the path of the willing burden bearer, the light of an eye seeing the rights of the slave as the rights of the prince, one and equal forever; the spring of a heart that would love his fellow man as his God and God as his fellow man; the patience of one who could wait 1900 years for a world to accept his offer and go free, only those who now drop the shackles of human existence and let the Mighty One bear away their sins and their sorrows, unquestioning why or how, but saying, "Yea, verily," only such can find.

"See thou: tell no man," saith he. How can we tell the mystic science of vicarious atonement for heartache, and death and the scourges of destiny?

Inter-Ocean Newspaper February 24, 1895

LESSON IX

The Raising Of Lazarus

John 11:30-45

The wonder science which Nettesheim says so few have studied during all time is the missing fourth dimension in space. Bodies are long, broad, thick, and, another dimension. Where have men laid it? It is the Lazarus of the home. With this dimension in practical running order every individual being everywhere would be independent of every other being and none could break through that final protection to make him afraid.

Little he would risk if England held the country's bonds with long-headed intention to own his fatherland as she got ownership of Egypt, for he would know how to evade the bullets of her warships and slide out of the prison vaults she would like to starve him into. He would even know how to live in plenty under his own vine and fig tree, securely fearless if the planet Mars had learned how to drop mildew and drought on his earth.

This lesson deals with the resurrection of and the life eternal of that dimension. It is the Jesus Christ type of man that understands it. The church has wept in vain. That is Martha. The laboring classes have wept in vain. They are Mary. But outside the city that holds church and people is a class of men and women with their eyes set heavenward. Down over their vision is falling a new power. With this power they will penetrate the darkness that covers the supporting, the cheering, the protecting principle, and there shall be no more death nor mourning.

The quality that keeps things alive is their touch of the fourth dimension in space, which has nothing in common with length, breadth, and thickness, though it always accompanies them. Many a man has held sway by virtue of his untaught contact with this unknown presence. It was untrained skill which tipped Paganini's bow with inimitable tones. It was uninstructed faculty which invented the microscope. It was unguided genius which released the secret virtue in the salt at Jericho.

Jenny Lind struck the heaven-descending dimension and with matchless genius strung the enraptured heartstrings of multitudes. For brief moments they felt the resurrection and the life of their laid-away memories of heaven. They were never the same people afterward.

Search the Scriptures Diligently

Abraham Lincoln struck the mystic dimension with his unexampled spirit and strung a world's heartstrings to the chord of omnipotent compassion. Never again can Czar or President ignore the cry of a people in undisturbed complacency. A world shall be prompt to know a discord in the Czar's manifesto and the President's commandments.

It was by gazing on the border lands of the unknown dimension that Moses and Solomon and Joshua and Paul and John gathered lessons in living which abide on the tablets of time unbroken. It is by feeding where they fed, touching the everlasting principle that they touched, that what they wrote is able to lay hold of the bound-up existence of man and set him free from the earth.

When the Scriptures are read, if we get no lifting up, it is wise to read them again. For while we abide in their length, breadth, and thickness, or the simply apparent, we cannot hear the crack of the hands that hold us in earthly straits equal to those which bound Lazarus. It is the inspiring radiance of the mystery their writers were leaning upon which makes their texts explain every man's lot, backward and forward.

Notice the thirty-fourth verse of John 11: *"And he said, where have ye laid him?"*

As an interpretation of this text for the daily light of millions of eager students, the wise men have written as follows: "Asked of the sisters, as a natural and courteous way of inviting them to lead the way to the tomb." (Page 71, Notes.) It will surely cause no offense to pronounce this explanation dry as sticks and dead as sawdust, when the text gleams on the mourning world at an hour like this to call their attention to the resurrection hour of the help they have missed.

Today what sounds smite the sweet airs of America but the wailings of Mary and Martha for buried support and protection? This is this day to be restored. There were mighty prayers ascending while two million Israelites toiled in bondage to Pharaoh, and down over the highways of those prayers came the delivering principle which not the armies and not the money of monarchy could withstand.

The Hour of Deliverance at Hand

When a lesson like this strikes on the heartstrings of a world under the famine whip of Russia and the sodden legislation of America it means that the hour of deliverance is here. The watch toward heaven for heavenly deliverance was never more intense than now all over the world. Whoever is looking heavenward for his help finds something within himself rising up and away from himself. This which rises up and away is his Jesus Christ quality. It will soon return to do unheard of miracles. "Where is that body laid which has been your support and protection? What was the name of that body?"

If the scriptures of our Christianity are worth anything it will not make any difference whether your famine is a money famine or a heart famine today, the hour of the resurrection of your lost help is come. Do you know what keeps your Lazarus down?

Do the people suppose that they can send upward for help and not have that help arrive? It has come. Make haste to leave your case to this world's shaking presence that stands on our earth. *"I am the resurrection and the life."*

Now is the time to give thanks that there is something more powerful than money, more powerful than friendly neighbors, more powerful than enemies, more powerful than death and the tomb. It is the descent of the light into the hardships of life and the up-springing of man's long hidden fourth dimension in space with its fearless energies. Welcome resurrection!

The hidden dimension is not limited in its applications. It can touch the fingers with new skill, so that they can open prison doors. It can touch the breath with new strength so that it is a sheath of safety from swords and guns. It can rouse the stones to disclose bread and the winds to disclose new virtues.

Health Deathless Although Buried

How hopelessly buried was the health of those thousands of incurables in Klosterle, 1753, when Gasner's upward gaze falling down through their tumors rose again as new bodies. The physicians had studied the length, breadth, and thickness of their swellings but not the other dimensions. How hopelessly buried was the freedom of our Southern blacks till the down gleaming God power rose again through the shocks of war for their sakes. How hopelessly dead seems brotherly consideration in our day when man deals out law and finance, and hides the grains and the coals from his fellow man. Hopelessly hidden in the vaults of the syndicates seems the money of a befooled people.

But that which Gasner did for the buried but deathless health of a multitude is now being done for the hidden but deathless brother love with its strength that does, indeed, seem so dead in the heads of state and business.

When the French people struck the nobles who had so long held their money under lock and key, how gladly the nobles would have peaceably given it up. But it was too late. Only by paying the penalty of their greed, would need be satisfied. But that was not the Jesus Christ restoration of the people's rights. That was the law of conduct and consequence operating in all its violence. That which is falling down into the nobles' hearts of our time, hardened as they seem with their quadruple copper-plated stay in the ground of inhuman business methods, is not law, as books and preachers have meant by law, trying to teach all men to do like the nobles, but a drawing forth heat that will melt every obstacle without revenue.

*"For lo! the days are hastening on,
By prophet-bards foretold."*

Every heart knoweth what lies buried, and this that lies buried is that Lazarus whom this Jesus Christ power now raiseth up by the quickening cords of the unknown force. The nations know their own buried Lazarus, and that Lazarus is now being raised up by this Jesus that now standeth in our midst. Lincoln struck on the world's compassion strings but this one strikes on the world's power strings.

Power of the Resurrection

That which is most powerful in man under the throbbing touch of the terrible Jesus now here is that which now rises. Some say that the great power that is now rising from the tomb of time is love. But, no, it is not love. Some say that the greatest power that can rise in the common heart of all men is brotherly consideration.

But, no, it is not brotherly consideration. Some say that that which is rising as the greatest — the Lazarus of this hour on the wings of the fourth dimension in space is peace. But, no, it is not peace. Some say it is prosperity that is the bound Lazarus to rise again for Martha arid Mary. But, no, it is not prosperity.

Stand back skies and waters, hide sun and moon and earth, ye have names by which ye may be called, but this which cometh up through the length, breadth, and thickness of the known and the names is unknowable, and hath no name except to such as Jesus Christ alone. "I am the resurrection." Under the sound of such a voice thy prosperity will rise, but that which raiseth it up is not prosperity. And a greater than prosperity ariseth.

Under the tread of such a foot the earth that binds thy health shall quake and rend, and thy health shall rise up, but that which raiseth it up is greater than health, and that which is greater than health cometh with it. Under the eye of this one a new life shall be given to this Nation, but that which raiseth up this life shall be greater than the life and a greater than life cometh up. The neighbors had seen sight resurrected (verse 17); they thought of health resurrected, but of this which is today arising nobody wotteth (knows).

Man's Quest for that Which Eludes

That which is being raised was never known to man. It was never in his charge. It hath been his eager quest forever, but forever it hath eluded him. Each taste of its mystic splendor vouchsafed him hath entranced him with love and wonder, but that taste was not lasting. Each contact with its mighty radiance hath made him divine in genius, but his genius hath not lasted. But now it springeth up, called by the voice of him that standeth in our earth, King of kings and Lord of lords, with death as powerless where he says "live" as the church hath been powerless where death hath said "die."

Do the people suppose that the ages can hurry on forever with famine after famine, and greedy nobles after nobles succeed, while some there are among us who know that "Jesus Christ" is the name that hides within its two-leaved hulls the majesty of Jehovah the comforter?

The holy ghost whom the Father will send in my name, shall teach you all things, and call all things to your remembrance.

Have the people, the Marys, and the churches, the Marthas, no confidence in the present quickening of the royal touch of that death and famine-conquering name whose outer sound is two words of eleven letters, but whose rending glory is manna for the hungry which none can take away, and help for the helpless which no law can wrest away, and comfort for the comfortless which death and hell and hate and darkness cannot hide?

"Said I not unto thee that if thou wouldst believe thou shouldst see the glory of God?"

But, whether we believe or not, it is now too late to mention. That which standeth in our midst shaking the earth with its heart-piercing wonder worketh the resurrection of the hidden power of which all the genius of greatest benefactor and delight of man heretofore hath been but symbol, and neither doubt nor complaining can hinder.

"For before the day was I am he, and there is none that can deliver out of my hand."

"It is decreed that earth
   From this time even forth
Shall rise, forever rise,
   Through all eternities
Borne in wondrous chariot
   From Paradise."

Inter-Ocean Newspaper March 3, 1895

LESSON X

The Rich Young Ruler
Mark 10:17-27

By the continued sounding forth of metaphysical speculations many discredited facts of past times have been proved genuinely possible. Though Oriental religion has forwarded to our doors as yet no adept of mystic phenomena who could even climb an impoverished tree, still it is credited that on the open square in Agra the mango rises from nowhere into plain sight and the solemn-eyed Yoghis crawl up ropes drawn from cosmic nothingness.

Persistent attention to occult phenomena on the part of the willfull, breezy Occident, for about twenty years, has now resulted in producing children of a marvelous order. The numberless musical prodigies are well enough as illustrations of this fact, but the children who can speak foreign languages without instruction are better. And still better is the child in Louisiana who is able, by putting out her little hands, to draw tables and chairs toward her without touching them.

Van Helmont declared that all men have these same magical powers stored within them, but know not how to use them, and have heretofore desisted from using them because they were once by somebody pronounced to be inheritances from Satan and not from heaven. It was metaphysics which first proclaimed that "all power is heavenly power, for there is no Satanic presence."

Whoever wrote the history of the acts of the disciples of Jesus intimates that acquaintance with Jesus uncovered this principle of useful attractiveness in mankind, for they found themselves drawing languages from etheric archives and claiming believers in their doctrines by these languages, of which they had previously known nothing.

In the story of Jesus as told by different eye witnesses he is related to have uncovered his heaven-born magical powers so perfectly that the dead rose out of their graves at his call, and manna hastened from its hiding places in the atmospheric globules .

In today's lesson, Mark, 10:17-27, a rich young man comes running after him, and, kneeling at his feet, calls him "Good Master."

All things Come to Jesus

Things which run up after this magical power in children seem to cling to them with loving attraction. Languages which come trooping to them sound sweet as music. Tables and chairs nestle in peaceful satisfaction. It was the sublime superiority of Jesus that morals and intellect came hurrying to do him homage, as well as life and bread. This time it is money and nobility, morals, intellect, youth, strength, manliness.

"How can we endure forever, embodied in this one man?" they asked. What was his answer?

"Be nothing."

"What for?"

"That that which hath dominion over morality, youth, intelligence, and strength may be all."

"Why cannot it have dominion and we still show ourselves forth to the admiring gaze of the world?"

"Because health, life, morality, which love the admiration of the world, must obey the world's commandments of thou shalt not and thou shalt, but the new man that riseth from being nothing is himself authority over what shall and what shall not be."

This is the case where Jesus took the free will of the world vicariously and forever healed all men who would watch him in Perea of wanting any will opposed to the heavenly light. In Perea he also healed mankind of pride of goodness. Here also he healed them of pride of birth, beauty, health, powerfulness; yea, he healed mankind of health and life itself.

All the luggage of will, pride of birth, learning, morality which men have carried since that time have been unnecessarily assumed.

It is noticed that the ego who lugs death lets go of it gladly when he realizes that Jesus Christ took death once for him and he need never die. He also lets go of sickness and deformity with great lightness of heart. But when he lets go of his beauty, his intelligence, his wealth, and will on the ground that Jesus took his will and wealth, his beauty and wit once for him, and he hath no need of them, he flinches.

The Realization of the Ego

The ego, carrying around so many treasures under the law of mutation and ending, wanted to keep those treasures forever. The ego in all mankind realizes that there is a way to be beautiful forever, healthy forever, intelligent forever. This ego is opposed to the law of time and change, but it is only under this realm of law of time and change that health, beauty, and intelligence are praised. This realm of law is sometimes called "the world." It is sometimes called "prince of this world." It is sometimes called "nature."

To the Jesus Christ man it is nothingness. It has no power. The ego which bundles itself up with law of time and change took for its first swaddling band "free will."

This "free will" it is a great strain for it to lay down again, consequently to be healed of "free will" is the crowning cure of man which Jesus Christ undertook.

In the case of the rich young man marched up on Mark's wonderful pages he is told as an ego lugging about things that are praised in this realm of law that in heaven, where the "poor" is God, these things are not praised.

It is the bread and meat of beauty and morality to praise them. It is the swelling pride of the ego wrapped up in health and wealth that it is praised for its wrappings as though it had made them. It is the terror of the ego of man that the wealth and health he had made are so fleeting.

"May there not be a teaching I can investigate that will keep me praised forever!"

"No. In the realm where I dwell nobody is praised. Nothing is praised. To praise is subtle intimation that there is something somewhere that is not worthy of praise."

Thus, Jesus Christ, by taking unto himself the world disease of love of praise, and even praise itself, offers man freedom from a blinding, binding pain which he has borne so long that to feed it and pamper it he calls the object of existence.

It was the wrapping bands of Lazarus which the "free will" must lay off. It was free will itself that Jesus took, as the representative of all men, and laid it down at the gate of heaven once so perfectly for all men, even taking their sorrow at giving it up, that by accepting his bearing of our "free will," and even our sorrow in giving it up, we are free of will and its unheavenly states of health, strength, and wealth, which are fleeting because they feed on praise.

To be healed of human existence at its most flourishing state was stated by Jesus as our finer healing than healing from death and the tomb. To be healed of will was his final idea of health. "The young man went away sorrowful." But he was healed. The Jesus man stood in his place bearing all his human existence. It is commonly interpreted that Jesus failed on this case; but common interpretation is a disease spreading over Christianity like a scab.

Common interpretation gives the character of Jesus from beginning to end as a failure. It makes him chief among a band of martyrs for truth. But Jesus was a more stupendous character than a martyr for truth. He understood the principle of healing by taking diseases into his own system and there annulling them for a whole world. He understood health, strength, beauty, intelligence, and powerful will, to be pleasurable diseases in the same sense as palsy, weakness, foolishness, deformity are disagreeable diseases. He taught loosing man utterly from this world. "In the world but subject to nothing in it." This was his plan of redemption.

Whoever tried to set forth, as hell alone from which the Messiah would deliver man, has the grave clothes of this world thick upon him. It is this world that he meant man to accept his offer of redemption from. This world at its heights of pleasure; this world at its depths of woe. "I will give you rest."

Jesus the Divine Healer

He who would interpret this section as proving Jesus a failure at healing from the world's crowning disease because the young man is represented as going away sorrowful needs to understand that his utter going away with his sorrow, leaving Jesus bearing all his will and its sorrow at dethronement, was Mark's masterly stroke in description of a finer healing than the healing of Lazarus. For the rich man became all Jesus.

This "finer" was not in the sense of more admirable but in the sense of more nearly the final cure. Nearer the treasures of heaven. He who is cured of his free will is on his own throne. Whoever thinks he has to work out his life by living it, bearing it, doing his faithful duty by it, is just as far from touching the magical purpose and power of Jesus as the one who wrote these lines on human life:

> "Must Jesus bear the cross alone,
>   And all the world go free?
> No, there's a cross for every one,
>   And there's a cross for me."

It was the cross of human existence setting up its will against heavenly existence, which Jesus carried once for all men, leaving their burden light; so lightly they could only rest from their labors while their work should follow them.

What a common, defeated, unadorable life to look upon as a God man on earth would the man of Nazareth be if there were no supernal principle of transplantation of other men from commonness of earth life by reason of his office on earth.

The Man of No Will

But there is another way of bearing the cross of Christ than by wearing the hardships of our daily lot bravely. There is another way of bearing the cross of Christ Jesus, as purposed by himself, than wearing the life and intelligence and prosperity of our daily lot with pleased gratitude. There is a freer man than the man of free will. It is the man of no will. It is the man who feels the hurt of laying down his will, but goes away into the agreement that the office of the God man was at the Perea point to take the free will of all men and leave man as entirely de-willed as the absolute and eternal One himself.

The most excruciating sorrow is yielding up free will. But will is a disease, even at its noblest choosing. What ability hath it to manufacture the absolute eternal God?

The assumption of all men's will with clear understanding of what to do with it was and is the Jesus Christ office on earth. The assumption of man's riches at their shroudings folds of health and honors, with the clear understanding of what to do with them, was the office of Jesus Christ on earth.

This lesson sounds the heavenly chords of man's noblest kindness to man as the doctrine of the closing circle of acceptance of the offer of one man for all men.

It is the closing segment of one majestic consciousness making the circle from heaven through earth and into heaven again. When any man accepts the offer that Jesus bear his cross of shame and defeat once, and now by that once borne cross he goes free of shame and defeat, he is not by that acceptance any more than half around the offered service. There is the other half of his burden to lay off on the burden-bearing presence still close at his hand.

<u>Discredited Principle of Possibility</u>

He who letteth go his pain and death must let go of his peace and life also.

By penetrating beyond the mind of pride or sorrow-freighted Bible commentator, and by acceptance of a grander purpose than showing other men how to bear pain bravely, we now sell all that we have even to will at its ablest, and give to the poor, viz: to that which hath no will, so destitute is it of earth characteristics; we arise free from earth forever; we accept the so called impossible; we disappear as obedience and appear as authority — this is the magic transformation foreshadowed by occult mysteries investigated by occidental boldness.

This is what the Perean episode compels the mind un-hypnotized by the dogma of individual suffering to see. It is what it compels one to see who refuses to be hypnotized by the subtle delightsomeness of free will. It is what everybody must accept who has accepted the unburdening of his sickness and sin, refusing to bear what has been once borne so well.

This is one of the discredited principles of possibility rousing up from the archives of eternity. We come up by our lightness of burden. What elysian miracles are wrought yet we labored not! With such a God as Jesus revealed all things are possible. "Yet will I magnify my name through thy works."

Inter-Ocean Newspaper March 10, 1895

LESSON XI

Zaccheus The Publican

Luke 1:10

The astrologer who predicted the career of the present Chief Executive and the state of the country while he should be shooting geese and otherwise diverting himself has now foreseen for this whole planet a cataclysm into which it is destined shortly to plunge, and nothing is to be left of the present order. Not a vestige of these former things shall remain to mark the exit of a memory.

If one is poised enough on the platform of his own judgment he will be able to see that the stars are the material record books before and behind both of men and worlds. He will know them as symbols of spiritual movements. Symbols are as accurate as mathematics. They can record times and seasons. They are the goats on the left of the throne.

Spiritual movements have never notified us of their times of arrival and departure, for there is no time in spirit. "The times and the seasons no man knoweth." They are as sure to take place with the mind of a race when they are discovered, as are the symbols of them to take place with the physical body of a race. They are the sheep on the right of the throne.

To be poised on the throne of the judgment seat in ourselves is to know spiritual movement for all their worth, and to know symbols for all their worth also. Daniel of old, a prisoner in Babylon, could calculate dates and cataclysms by the logic of symbols, and could also read the spiritual precursors of them which have no dates.

He foretold what should be operating on the spiritual heavens in these days that would be throwing the stars on the material heavens out of their orbits and dropping the earth into doom. He could see that it was because Michael should be standing up, "that great prince who standeth for my people." Whoever is watching the signs of the times sees plainly that from the material standpoint there can be nothing but vortex for the planet. But the Bible stories record the spiritual signals which shall be flying at such a crisis. Even the lesson selected by the International Committee for today points to what is now and what shall be.

Lesson Taught by Zaccheus' Guest

Zaccheus had lived by the business principles of the nineteenth century. Logically he saw a cataclysm ahead of himself because of them. But he climbed a sycamore tree to watch for a "Michael" to stand for him. This Michael was on the way. "I will abide in thy house today," he said.

The effect of having this "Michael" in his house was such that he wanted to disgorge all the money he had drawn from the people. He wanted to pay them interest on it.

But take notice, Jesus Christ had not mentioned money matters. He had not even thought of them. When Zaccheus swung himself from a thriving business man to a broad-gauge philanthropist it was in consequence of fastening his eyes on the wonderful guest in his house, but not because his guest was treating him to unload. The guest in his house was not occupying himself with those two poles of a magnet called honesty and dishonesty. He was on the throne of the neutral center, not overjoyed, at generosity, not filled with gloom at selfishness.

When Zaccheus had swung the pendulum of his mind as far as the limits of the sheep side of authority he hit the cataclysm to goodness and badness. He suddenly struck salvation from them both. — (Luke 14:9)

There is no salvation like salvation from polar opposites. How the ages have rolled by waiting for the precious argon in the atmosphere to have the two-leaved gate, oxygen and hydrogen, swing open right and left to show its uncompanioned face. How innocently it operates to burn up the books on chemistry and start up an entirely new science to stand for the people, perhaps even to showing paupers how to twist silver threads out of cold snaps and gold nuggets out of fogs. How worthless will be the banker's gold when he cannot use it for a weapon to domineer over his neighbors.

There are other things than stars which are now prophesying changes for mankind. And there are things on the symbol side of existence which promise a Michael to stand up in the house of business — bruised humanity. And we can tell by these material things just how near us is the Michael whose neutral presence is to make such havoc with our good actions on the one hand and our bad actions on the other.

Importance of the Fourth Dimension

He is just as near as the actual understanding of the fourth dimension in space which is what has to be hit accidentally or knowingly to make any project successful.

A singer may have all the vocal chords in perfect trim and have paid thousands for the cultivation thereof, but unless he hits that fourth dimension his singing is wooden. So of a book, so of a speaker. The fourth dimension is the "success dimension." Just as near as we are to understanding it so near are we to Michael, our deliverer. Let no man think he understands it till he has by knowing touch of it restored his teeth and his intelligence to their proper bases and by knowing how to touch it again has found himself independent of smiles and frowns.

Michael is just as near mankind perched in the sycamore tree of watching for something new with wonderful help in it as mankind is near the wise use of that angle in movements which makes a child strong as a horse; just as near as the free use of argon, as near as man has seen into his own soul, as near as he has come to rupturing the etheric atom and disclosing the neutral substance around which the forces of nature are swinging.

On the material side all these are powers threatening absolute changes to old orders. And on the spiritual side there is prophesy of some man, or some principle, or some nameless knowledge coming forward which shall as utterly overthrow former standards of morals and religion as Zaccheus was relieved of dishonesty and honesty. Astrology and revelation go hand in hand. In this Bible story which hits the fourth dimension in space at every new angle Zaccheus suddenly disappears, leaving only the neutral center visible. So the Sabbath day accusers all disappeared; so the rich man disappeared; so Zaccheus, who particularly stands in this section for humanity at large believing in badness on one hand and goodness on the other.

Watch the Soul Center

In each of us there is a soul center which never swings any man into satisfaction with his honesty any more than into satisfaction with dishonesty. There is a way of watching this soul center that causes it to reform a bad man, but it does not know anything about his badness. Watching it reforms a man of goodness just as surely.

The Bible stories all refer to the effect of watching this soul. Jeremiah shows the effect upon Elisha the Tishbite. He had touched the neutral center of his own being sufficiently to affect an army with blindness which started to do him harm, yet he touched them not; and to stop the famine of Samaria though he only looked once toward it after gazing long at the moveless eternal that abode in his house.

Luke makes Jesus the carpenter so poised on the throne of his own center that he can overcome the world one moment and be overcome by the world the next moment without shaking his balance. Without doubt Matthew, Mark, Luke, and John depict the effect absolute, which crying the indifferent soul at the headquarters of being will have upon us better than Esdras depicts it by the story of Moses, and better than Badeau by the story of Grant. The more one watches his own soul the less power there is in pain to hurt him and the less power there is in pleasure; the less notice he takes of dishonesty, the less he is pleased with uprightness. And every man is more or less of the Zaccheus type which is a mixture of Simon and Judas. Simon wants to reform the world of its badness. He mourns over evil even to the fighting pitch. Judas wants gain at any cost but he and Simon are alike disquieted. Neither the reformer who mourns nor the business man who shuts his eyes, is comfortable.

Zaccheus Not a Clean Type

Zaccheus is not a clean type. He is a mixture. But as he plays Judas and is miserable, he plays Simon and is just as miserable. Neither one has struck his own center. The four gospels show what kind of a man you will exhibit when you stand at your own center. You will not be trying to reform the world. Yet the world will change where you are. You will not be trying to upset the happiness of the good man; yet he will be everlastingly pointing his skinny finger to some heavenly future where he is to be happy. Finally they will both stop talking and maneuvering and look your way. As you are not watching them, but are poising on your own neutral center, they will catch that poise by knowing you, and you will be doing exactly what Luke says that Jesus was doing. Daniel called him Michael. The Oriental farther east than Babylon and Judea, called him Buddha.

You may call the neutral center by whatever name you like. You may even call it Satan. It will not hear. Its office is that of affecting, not of being affected. You may scold at it for not making more haste with dissolving you as mind and matter. It will not heed. But the loss of your mind is as sure as the loss of your avoirdupois. You are bound for salvation when you notice that this day the soul of you abides in your house.

If you can point to some man who has had his omnipotent center more exposed than Jesus Christ, you will find that pointing his way will make you resemble him in the way you affect reformers like Simon, and money getters like Judas, or both combined in one, like Zaccheus.

The more closely we take notice of a character the more we are drawn into likeness of him, whether we like him or not. How the peculiarity of the Jesus Christ of Luke is that as men take notice of him they change very rapidly, and suddenly find that they are not looking at a man of history at all, but at themselves. They find themselves rising lightly to the throne of some authoritative independence of everything material and everything mental. It is the precious wonder of argon that it swings oxygen to the right and hydrogen to the left and smiles in monatomic independence of them.

Michael Represents the Unmovable

So the Michael who standeth up for mankind today is any man who is not moved by mind or his body. And neither the destruction of matter nor the loss of elevation of mind hits him.

When the church watches Luke's Jesus it talks about the kind of a sycamore Zaccheus climbed and describes the darkness of the tomb Jesus was encased in. So by such talk we have maundered for centuries in length, breadth, and thickness, hitting only by dint of much effort against the other dimension which has nothing to do with tombs and taxes, yet which operates on them like water on salt.

The earth dissolves at the glance of Michael, to give all men a look at their own soul, which is their own defender and deliverer. Mind cannot think any more thoughts when once it stops still for any man to search around in himself for his own soul poise.

Notice that vision which you use when you look toward Jesus Christ now present in this universe, not tied to any spot. That vision is not mind. It is not eyeballs. Yet that vision is the strongest thing that accompanies you on your journey through life. Notice what vision you use when you search for the neutral center within your own being. You do not use your eyeballs, and you do not use your thought. Yet that vision toward your mighty standing place is the delivering principle. It is the faculty in you stronger than any array of events that might attempt to defeat you. It is the "Tao" or the "path."

Just as fast as you speed on the everlasting path toward the high and holy one that inhabiteth your eternity just as fast will men find the use of the uncompanioned potentiality in air and the happifying fourth dimension in space. And just so fast will the earth hurry toward her cataclysm. And just so fast will mind roll away like a scroll. And just so fast will mind and matter show that they have no laws that the Jesus Christ in man is bound to respect.

He tells the neutral center in the man what is wanted, and it happeneth as he saith. He makes and unmakes what it pleaseth him.

It is every man's privilege to cast his vision on his own un-companioned, un-contaminated poised center. It is every man's privilege to stand there in full authority over his whole lot in life.

When we wonder what makes up the difference between power and no power among the people, let us be heedful that power is not of matter or mind, but lies along the path or the "Tao" of the everlasting mystic vision always present. Whoever climbs toward it sees his own dominion be he slave or king. It is not a safe day for the material man when one enters on the mystic path. It is not a safe day for spiritual things when one enters on the mystic path. There is only the Michael left everywhere.

Notice how in all these stories Jesus is left as the only spokesman and only actor. And he always speaks of something of which no man was thinking. Last Sunday it was: "With God all things are possible;" today it is: "Save that which was lost." Salvation of the throne presence that has been lost sight of by the swings of mind with its multitudinous explanations and the swings of matter with its symbols.

The globe of all mind wheels to the right. The globe of all matter wheels to the left. "The Son of man is come." He is the sun of the new age. He is not a man, but the soul of all men. He riseth o'er the eastern horizon line shining in strength and beauty called by the watchers toward their own high and holy poised center of being. In such a light there is no need of the sun, so he fadeth. In such a smile there is no need of good and noble men, so they perish forever. In such a fire there can be no dry hearts unburned.

Enter the path, climb up the tree, gaze steadfastly toward the coming light. It has never shone unclouded on this world, but now it cometh. To make the nations prove the glory of his steadfastness, the wonder of his love.

Inter-Ocean Newspaper March 17, 1895

LESSON XII

Purity Of Life

Romans 13:8-14

There's a little book of axioms in mental science which no Occidental student has proved the accuracy of, and which no Orientalist yet wafted to our shores has been a living demonstration of, though the book was written in India no telling how long ago, and the faithful Westerners have been working hard at it now these dozens years.

There is one purpose running through the book, and that is to urge every man to get the strings on a singular apparatus called the mind. If once he can hinder the thoughts of that unruly engine and direct them at will, he has a masterly fine time riding over this globe. It shows that actions all spring from runaway thoughts if those acts are not easily controllable. For instance, if you cannot go without eating for six weeks or so without feeling faint you have attained to little or no management of your mental machinery.

One proof of your ability to handle the reins on your mind would be to lie still as a log in the forest showing no signs of breathing long enough for the birds to build their nests and hatch their young on your head and in your clothes without their discovering you to be anything but a warm tree-trunk.

As to-day's Bible lesson on purity of life suggests outward conduct and mental responsibility, and this book of metaphysical trainings is all about the same, it is well to compare the ideas of two disciples of two such similar masters of matter and mind as Gautama and Jesus.

First, if the author of the little old book was indeed as far from the quality of Gautama as Paul was from the quality of Jesus, then of course it is no wonder that not a yogi disciple of his who lands in New York can do a single one of the marvelous acts which the bona fide Gautamaite most certainly can, and that while the yogi repeats the metaphysics, already well known in the West, he, like Paul, is taking his smoking and his meat-eating up into his heavenly assertions.

Did anybody ever read between the lines anywhere that the mind of Jesus was contemplating such themes as Paul is forever hauling into his sermons! Thus the student of Paul can almost always be easily detected by his discourses on deportment — outward behavior.

He talks all the time about living the life. Then he enumerates what performances to abjure and what performances to tie to. But Jesus did indeed teach that *"because I live ye shall live also,"* and therefore wasted no time or breath in such verses as Romans 13:13. Knowing that the high and holy one that inhabiteth eternity was his own nature from beginning to end, he knew that to know him was to live his life.

Abstain from the Appearance of Evil

Notice that the discussion of today's theme must swing the attention from the globe of matter to the globe of mind, and from mind to physics back again. But who this one is that is attending to mental gymnastics and physical gyrations this Bible section only hints at, and one must read over the whole little book of aphorisms to find if its author were more interested in the one who is neither matter nor mind, or the gymnastics of matter and mind.

The golden text is: *"Abstain from all appearance of evil."* The fruit of this abstinence is to be a deeper state of sanctification. "Restraint of actions will lead to restraint of thought. This is being wholly sanctified," as he says in another verse.

Verse 9, of this chapter, turns one's gaze from behavior of body to behavior of mind. It is summed up as a great future for mankind when he has the lines on those two unruly terrors, namely, his physical constitution and his thinking apparatus. (Verse 10)

The author of the book of mental science written nobody can tell when, takes up Paul's verses in a somewhat different fashion. Read Paul to the Romans, 13:9-10 and then notice this author's idea. It reads this way; *"When abstinence from theft in mind and act is complete in the yogi, he has the power to obtain all material wealth."*

Paul says that there will be no ill to our neighbor when there is no stealing from his substance by our outward draughts on him and our mental tractions. Neither one of them makes the stealing business the effect, but institutes it as a cause. Jesus and Gautama taught that drawing my substance and my sustenance from the Almighty One, I would be above the system of haulage from my neighbors, either by the activity of my fingers and speech or my mentality. Both Gautama and Jesus knew better than to set for me so severe a task as abstaining from theft.

Both taught that the high and holy one that inhabiteth eternity is able to stop my mind from its tricks of planning how to get things, but no amount of restraining and punishing my planning and arranging habits will ever stop them. After ten thousand or so years of punishing themselves the Orientals much prefer the planning and contriving dodges of the

Western world in their getting of our Western dollars. The Jesus and Gautama doctrine was: *"Seek ye first the kingdom of God and all these things shall be added." "Depending on me thou shalt know me completely."*

You may take heed to one fact on this journey of attention to first the physical world and then the mental, and that is that the less a man is attentive to either of them the more mastery he has over them, provided that his attention is fixed on the one, whose ways are not bodily ways at their most sanctified conduct, nor mental reasonings at the height of their assertions.

Look Unto Me and Be Ye Saved

There is one forever present on all occasions whom to attend unto is life and health and power. Though we make our bed in adversity still nigh us is the Mighty One. "Look unto me and be ye saved." Though we be inclined, to the pleasures and cruelties of the senses of the flesh, still forever nigh us is the Mighty One. "Look unto me and be ye saved." Though the angers and loves and stealings and envies of an unruly set of thoughts are our portion, to the extent of a Nero, a Claudius, or a Loyola of Spain, still, never failing, never fainting, never changing, the One of whom Jesus and Gautama spoke is near. "Look unto me and be ye saved."

The Greeks had a name for this ever accompanying one. They called it the Self. Their highest motto was: "Know Thyself." The Persians had a name for this eternal comrade. They called it the "Light." They proclaimed that to watch that shining light would be to flee as a bird from the snares of human existence. Nehemiah, the Hebrew prophet, called the ever-present comrade of his life his "Self." John, the Hebrew lover of Jesus, called the eternal ally the "Light." *"I consulted with myself,"* said Nehemiah. *"There is a light that lighteth every man that cometh into the world,"* said John.

Paul says in verse 12, *"Let us put on the whole armor of light."* Then he tells us how to behave in order to get on that armor. He can never get on that armor by behavior though he should learn to hold his breath for a week at a stretch and abstain from calling names for a lifetime.

He says in verse 14, *"Put on the Lord Jesus Christ and make not provision for the flesh to fulfill the lusts thereof."* Here he calls the light by the name of one man who made so much provision for his flesh, judged from the flesh and mind trainers' standards that they called him a glutton and a wine-bibber, yet it injured not his Majesty, nor hindered his miracles.

The whole that a man is, in the greatness of his character or the freedom of his life, is measured by what he is looking at. People are astounded at the phenomenon of a concourse of intelligent men and women passing over and ignoring the sliding panels and ceiling strings with which a Blavatsky jerked down Koot Hoomi and Morya missives from the mystic plaster of a common house, but pouncing with merciless examinations upon the few well-done little imitations of the same practiced by a judge.

No System Majestic Enough to Watch

The secret lies in the direction of their attentions. One's gaze is on the mighty mysteries that hang over the heads of all men, and the other's is lifted no higher than the applause of humanity. It has been the amazement of multitudes that one who instituted a system of healing whereby name and fame and money were more than piled up was not ever cured by the system, and yet whoever else should attempt to promulgate it, having the same uncured bodily state, would be jailed for a fraud. The secret lies in the direction of their attentions. One has eyes set on the forces that swing the planets and men in their censers, while the others are set on the system itself.

No system is majestic enough to watch. The stars that wheel in solemn distance to the songs of beings out of the reach of imagination are not high enough to watch. The sparkling reasonings of a Plato are not safety enough to keep me from the clutches of a body that tempts my attentions, the terrors of a mind that cannot cope with the nineteenth century's Grand Rapids. Paul, with his forcing processes for thoughts and senses, has never yet saved a man from the stake in the days of stakes, and from the shameful ignominy in the days of competitive examinations.

The author of the aphorisms shall find his most faithful devotees too worn and discouraged to proceed; the lofty speculations to which people have been turning, for lo these many years are not any of them the one unto whom the gaze must turn that the body shall move in its safe beauty, unspoiled by passions and untouchable by appetites. They are not the high and holy One inhabiting eternity, whose smile on mind sets it to tunes of loving kindness caught from the land of the unexiled soul.

Let who will reason of life, light, and immortality strain the supple muscles of his great mind till he can trace the stars beyond Orion. As for me, I watch my God. Let who will starve and beat and hate and strive with his body, giving it the one precious pearl of priceless count, namely, his attention. I shall heed the counsels of one who stepped out of the grave and shone on the night of darkening asceticism and blackening philosophy with the splendor of his watch of the Eternal God. "What I say unto you I say unto all, watch."

Something Greater Than Rebuke

If Blavatsky watches the mysteries she shall laugh as free greatness in the faces of criticism. What she hath her eye on is greater than rebukes. But the occult mysteries are not the absolute and unchangeable ones upon which Jesus was looking when the tomb gave him up and the morning of time broke on man.

The reasoner, with shining descriptions of the all-good one, with life and not death in his dews, shall be greater and freer than the disputers who judge by sight of evil and death, but follow thou no system of thinking. The everlasting glory that walketh beside thee is not a system of thinking. Give the one priceless treasure thou carriest with thee, which is thy attention only, to the Thinkless One. So shall thy mind be glorious, unfailing wonder, full of stupendous powers, but thou didst not train it.

So shall thy body step forth in its beauty, the radiant sign of the last of pain, but thou didst not train it, for no man hath ever yet lived with any possible approachment to training power over his body. As long as Paul is understood as proclaiming a method which any man living can carry out, just so long will we see the poorhouse face the churchman indissoluble adjunct, and the jail stare the college in the eye — the undefeatable companion thereof.

The senses shall master thee long as thou lookest their way, and themes such as Paul often had on his lips must perforce be thine also. But Jesus Looked Godward, and his senses glowed till Revelation wrote them down as the bright and morning star pure with adorable divinity.

Words Which Shall Not Pass Away

Thy thoughts shall leap against thy happiness so long as thou lookest their way, and thou shalt weep over mistakes and misfortunes with the little sorrowful Dalai Lama till the sun sets on thy human destiny a withered, half-demented old sage. But Jesus Christ looked Godward, and though heaven and earth pass away his words shall not pass away, and the enchantment of his unconquerable smile shall endure forever.

It makes no difference from what part of this round earth they come with their postures and breaths and salts and sands and tiltings and fastings, the flesh profiteth nothing saith the man who understood them all for what they are worth. It makes no difference from what part of the round earth they come with their mutterings and formulas and memorizings and high languages and restraints of language and concentrations of mind — take no thought saith that one who understood them all for what they are worth. "Watch." Then shall mind break forth as the morning and thine health shall spring forth speedily. Then shall the new language spring to the lips of the nations. Then shall the Elohim sing on the hills of the ocean. "The night is far spent, the day is at hand," shouted Paul. Peering through the mists of nineteen hundred years of vain attempts at finding the Savior and Lover, through his foolish system, he caught the foregleam of a day when the world should hurl systems and philosophers and religions to one side, wide awake enough now to see that under their yokes we might go on and on and on in the silly belief that they would land us somewhere, but that, free from their yokes, we know that they have constituted the darkness of time. Light has come by turning to face One that never knew them. With one foot on the surging sea of mind, and one foot on the rolling lands of sense, the angel of this instant crieth that time shall be no more. There is no more attention to be given to the mind. One careth. Attend to that One. There is no more training of the life. Because I live, ye shall live."

Inter-Ocean Newspaper March 24, 1895

LESSON XIII

Review

Peter stands for instantaneous accomplishment. His eagle eye ranges backward and rapidly takes all the main events into this moment's page. He can see forward and compel what was intending to come to pass a long time from now to take place today. He says that the secret reason why churches are built is for cure after death. They adroitly teach that mankind are destined to a dreadful disease after death, and as prevention is possible, let us take it.

He teaches that when the Jesus Christ name of the Deity has reached the quick of its potentiality there will be no competition of man against man. He teaches that pretty nearly everything that is done on this earth is done by the human will. He shows that when the human wills stops still and lets the divine operation be visible every city and every church steeple will disappear. A new city with temples not built by hired labor will be disclosed. It already lieth foursquare in our midst, but as we are flashing the shadowy glitterings of our personal determinations against it, we do not see it.

Something is going to happen about these days which is to stop the wild determinations of each human being to have his own way and domineer over somebody or something. He will be glad to stop trying. He will see that by projecting his will over his affairs he has hidden what was in them for his life, he will stop being strong-willed. He will not urge affairs to do what he wants. He will learn that affairs have glorious news for him all by themselves. In returning from stretching your will, and rest from thinking about your destiny, says Zachariah, shall you be satisfied,

To Dorcas who had exercised her will to death, Peter said: "Rise!" To Aeneas, who had tired his mind to paralysis, he said: "Be well!" Each of the twelve men circulating around Jesus stands for something special. The Jesus man is the pivotal center in all things. The twelve disciples of Jesus are the twelve powers that fold up like gates around some men and open wide in one or two particulars in others.

The story of Jesus Christ is the story of one man who lived from within, straight from his divine center, and thus exhibited all the twelve powers in perfection. He could do everything. He knew everything. He therefore knew better than to operate a human will over his daily lot, and he knew better than to manage his life by his thoughts. Returning toward his central fire he dwelt in heaven every day. He brought from that fire a quality with him, and shed it over everything he looked at. His eyes had awful majesty in them. His breath imbued with supernatural energy. His hands had life-giving forces. His very clothing shed an aura of enchantment. Words broke open like golden bottles, and disclosed potencies which other men could not make them disclose because they knew not the secret of breaking them open.

Magical Essences Within Words

Mary Howett, the poetess, discovered the magical essences hidden within words. She knew not how to break them open and pour out their essences. She must know what Jesus of Nazareth knew to do that. He found the covered-up virtues in clay, in saliva, in water, in salt. Elisha had been accounted a wonder because he had discovered the magical essential in salt nine hundred years before. "No man could do these things that thou doest except God be with him!" exclaimed a ruler of the Jews, when he heard of the miracles wrought by him that had all the irresistible force of Elijah, the sweet miraculousness of Elisha, the noble wisdom of Solomon, the spiritual melody of David, focused into himself.

Then he caught greater and hotter glories from his own hearth-fire of divinity. He returned toward the "I am" of himself so often that when his voice sounded on the airs of Palestine, its echoes, rolling from soul to soul down the centuries, broke open like sunny globules of Elixir on all who stopped to listen. Even today the airs are entrancing with life and health. Even today they are charged with melting tenderness. Even today they bear away in their dissolving forgetfulness the hurts of a world.

Elijah raised the Zarephath's child, Elisha raised the Shunammite's boy, but Jesus Christ raiseth thee. Time cannot dull the enchantment of the breath of divinity; hard labor cannot bow the shoulders of the burden carrying presence; the competition of man against man to get away so the places and breads of life, cannot hinder the conquering instant now breaking.

"Heaven and earth will pass away but I live forever." It became apparent to the one bloom of humanity flowering from the sublimest in all men of all ages that he could take the human existence of a planet, the life and death, the ignorance and wisdom of all creation, what had been, what shall be, and what is, and be it all in himself. It became apparent to him that he could offer it all in his own self to the central sun of his life, which he saw was the same sun in all men shining alike. He did it. On the records of time no precedent lay before him to prove that this was a possibility. Friends had to falter, and foes had to exult while he was taking the loneliness of all men born and unborn into his bosom, to bear toward the throne of his own central God,

which he saw was the central God in all men alike. But he did it.

Study ye the radiant stars, but they will not bring healing light in the night of adversity. Study ye the ministering seraphs speeding to and fro, but they cannot be found when the world hath set its heel on hope and home. Know ye not that Jesus Christ represents what man is empowered to be and is kindled to accomplish when he makes the study of the central "I am" his sole business?

"Let death come on, I am the resurrection. Let the darkness hide, I am the light. Let the sun go down and the earth rend and the temples fall, I have prepared heaven for you, O world, that hath known me as coming, and world that remembers that I have been here!"

The Greatness of Man's "I Am"

This is the power and greatness of the "I Am" in all men. But the Peter exercise of the "I am" at the axis of man is the quickness with which a word exhibits itself. The Thomas quality of the "I am" is the riches of indiscretion. It sounds well to be called discreet. It looks sensible to be careful of your reputation, but the "I am" rushing through you is as indifferent to what people will think or say of you, as Thomas broken down. Peter was once all positive in error and formulated the hard rocks of his assertions on the dark side. He said carelessly, "I don't know!" and in no time at all his words marbleized into situations which were too hard for him. He said: "I see the visibility of God" and his words founded a mighty church.

Thomas cared nothing, whether his religious comrades were disgusted at his discretion. He cared nothing when his religious comrades or the world at large thought him beaten in argument. First he did care for his social and secular reputation for gullibility; then he cared nothing and this made him rich. Rich in energy. Plenty of men today have genius, riches, opportunity, to set the light of the higher gospel of the dawning age in plain sight of the world by some one move that would cast their reputation at the first step and glorify their name at the next, but they hug the fleeting chimera of discretion.

Careful Melanchthon, indiscreet Luther! The Archbishop of Zante declared the principle that "divinity point in all men alike is identical," to be absolute truth, but dangerous to teach the masses. He who keeps his eyes set toward his own central "I am" till he strikes the Jesus Christ understanding, will come forth one day the supremely indiscreet in conduct, with the energy of a Jesus. The lion of the tribe of Judah does not care for the rats of slander. To him it is easy to be called a glutton, a winebibber, an associate of the ostracized. When the shags of opinion are viewed in the noonday of posterity it is the wonder of science how the geniuses of the morning missed the kernel of what was transpiring, and muled round on what society and college might think.

Could Nero have seen where the Christians would land on the shores of a day yet to be, he would have thrown the flatteries of pagan comrades to oblivion and honored the Christians instead of burning them in his gardens.

Could the chief prosecutor of Galilee have foreseen the greatness of his prisoner's coming name he would have set him in state for all men to take note of. Could Booth have foreknown Lincoln he would have bared his bosom for the glorious name's sake. Could man of today foresee where the science of the equal God in all men shall stand he would give all that he hath to help make it known. Let him that hath a great fame for piling up millions at the expense of his neighbors once see how the Jesus Christ man within himself would do, and he would buy up the coal mines and throw them open for men to share, as the heart of love means them to share while the sun shines on the mountains. And that is what some great indiscreet Thomas exercise of the Jesus power is going to do to hide the bauble of discreet falling in with the times.

To Recognize the Yoke of Christ

The twelve men of Jesus each represent some one human trait melted under the fire of divine man. Under the yoke of the human characteristic life was a hard road to travel.

"With that yoke melted, prisons and famines and scourgings and stonings become nothing." Therefore the golden text of this review lesson is, "Yoke my yoke upon you." So light is the burden laid by the divinity in man on his shoulders, that he does not even know that back of him is such a yoke. Let him turn. *"A man shall be satisfied from himself,"* said Solomon. He means from his own altar fire.

In reviewing the signals by which each may recognize the yoke of the Jesus Christ at our heart's core, we are told by the International Committee to take a map and put on Palestine's sea a ship, to remember the journey of Jesus just begun; a well of some sort for his footsteps to Sheahem; a cradle and a star for Bethlehem, sands for the wilderness place, a cup for Cana, etc.

These represent the outward path of the son of Mary. He had another path which he took. That was with his mind. He looked over the human experience of a world. He said that there was no kind of study of it that would ever amount to anything. He found that careful observations of the precession of the equinoxes, even to predictions of eclipses, had not saved mankind from the yoke of human nature, though they had been watched for ages; that the discovery of geometry and trigonometry, the calculi, the square of the hypotenuse, the decimal system, and the faces of triangles had not brought the like yokes of life for which the ages had groaned; that close attention for generations to the volumes of gas that ride in inverse ratio through the ethers proportionate to the pressures they support had been of no use in the hour of friendless age; that grammar at the richness of the timeless Sanskrit had no life in it; that music with its much practiced tones on the streets of history had not healing power for the heart of the widow of Nain; that lacey minarets and Greek hemicycles of beauty could do nothing; therefore "the kingdom of heaven cometh not by observation," was his bold assumption.

Whoever receives the doctrine that heavenly happiness comes not by outward observation makes a sharp turn from what he has been believing. This is John the Baptist having his head cut off. Titian out has pictured Salome with the head of John the Baptist on a charger. Anything which I believe will make the kingdom of heaven manifest but which I soon see will not do so is a principle cut short. Have you thought that swinging your thoughts up to the affirmation of "God is love" would make heaven come on earth? Well, it will not. Turn and see the starting point of yourself and then you will only say, "God is love" when it will work instantaneously.

Truth Must Come From Within

You may admire the picture by Titian, but how much of heaven on earth sings out from the canvas? You may like the tinkle of the words, "God is love," but the church has not seen her repetitions of them warm the commercial methods of this unworthy and awful civilization. Nothing that swings on the land or the sea is worth while till it is seen by eyes lit at the soul of yourself. Nothing that reasons of the changeless eternal, though so glittering that it dazzles like Veda Vyasa and Plato, has come from the altar fire, till you have stopped reasoning and asserting and tipped your tongue with the flame that burns in your heart. Then, like Peter, your reasonings will convert 3,000 in one day. Peter is the Jesus word that throttles time. But he drags in the fish nets of ages, repeating and repeating till he faces Jesus.

Christian science and the Catholic Church, one and inseparable, now and forever, repeating and repeating, with eyes cast out over the faces of men and dynasties, expecting and expecting, because of the formulating power of words!

Let them stop. Let them turn. At the heart of all men standeth Jesus Christ, the flame of omnipotent heavenly authority. One look that way and then take notice of the suddenness with which Peter of the fishnets of formulas was melted into Peter the living demonstration of the instantaneousness of the actual Jesus power.

One look that way and one faculty you will get hot with will be the ability to disclose quickly what heavenly tenderness foldeth you round. But your ministry will not stop with detecting your own protected and powerful life. Whatever you tell the people of this world about the protecting and prospering and enlightening effect of the yoke of Jesus Christ they will feel promptly.

They see the authority vested in you to decree that the veils of flesh shall part and show them the realm that lieth four-square on this earth already.

Elisha was vested with authority to rend the veils of mortal wills and expose the strong hosts already to defend before Gehazi's sight. Stephen was vested with authority to rend the veils of sensation caused by human wills and mental determinations and to expose for himself what he must step into.

The hour cometh and now is when the recognition of his own standing place as the same authority that Jesus Christ meant to teach is such a recognition as acts at once and nothing can interfere. Under this dispensation he saith: "The yoke on the neck of me by the Me at my authoritative standing place is the yoke of authority. I have served under the yoke of obedience even to the lying down of all the twelve powers, that the central authority in me, whose present name is Jesus Christ, may exhibit the divine glory with which the true king reigns."

Inter-Ocean Newspaper March 31, 1895

Notes

Other Books by Emma Curtis Hopkins

- *Class Lessons of 1888 (WiseWoman Press)*
- *First Lessons in Christian Science (The Desert Church of the Learning Light)*
- *Bible Interpretations (WiseWoman Press)*
- *Esoteric Philosophy in Spiritual Science(WiseWoman Press)*
- *Genesis Series 1894 (WiseWoman Press)*
- *High Mysticism (WiseWoman Press)*
- *Self Treatments with Radiant I Am (WiseWoman Press)*
- *The Gospel Series (WiseWoman Press)*
- *Judgment Series in Spiritual Science (WiseWoman Press)*
- *Drops of Gold (WiseWoman Press)*
- *Resume (WiseWoman Press)*
- *Scientific Christian Mental Practice (DeVorss)*

Books about Emma Curtis Hopkins and her teachings

- *Emma Curtis Hopkins, Forgotten Founder of New Thought* – Gail Harley
- *Unveiling Your Hidden Power: Emma Curtis Hopkins' Metaphysics for the 21st Century (also as a Workbook and as A Guide for Teachers)* – Ruth L. Miller
- *Power to Heal: Easy reading biography for all ages* –Ruth Miller

To find more of Emma's work, including some previously unpublished material, log on to:

www.highwatch.org

www.emmacurtishopkins.com

WISEWOMAN PRESS

Vancouver, WA 98665
800.603.3005
www.wisewomanpress.com

Books Published by WiseWoman Press

By Emma Curtis Hopkins

- *Resume*
- *The Gospel Series*
- *Genesis Series 1894*
- *Class Lessons of 1888*
- *Self Treatments including Radiant I Am*
- *High Mysticism*
- *Esoteric Philosophy in Spiritual Science*
- *Drops of Gold Journal*
- *Judgment Series*
- *Bible Interpretations: Series I, thru XXII*

By Ruth L. Miller

- *Unveiling Your Hidden Power: Emma Curtis Hopkins' Metaphysics for the 21st Century*
- *Coming into Freedom: Emily Cady's Lessons in Truth for the 21st Century*
- *150 Years of Healing: The Founders and Science of New Thought*
- *Power Beyond Magic: Ernest Holmes Biography*
- *Power to Heal: Emma Curtis Hopkins Biography*
- *The Power of Unity: Charles Fillmore Biography*
- *Power of Thought: Phineas P. Quimby Biography*
- *The Power of Insight: Thomas Troward Biography*
- *Gracie's Adventures with God*
- *Uncommon Prayer*
- *Spiritual Success*
- *Finding the Path*

www.wisewomanpress.com

List of *Bible Interpretation Series,* with dates, from the First - the Twenty-second Series

This list is complete through the twenty second series. Emma produced twenty-eight *Series* of *Bible Interpretations.*

She followed the Bible Passages provided by the International Committee of Clerics who produced the Bible Quotations for each year's use in churches all over the world.

Emma used these for her column of Bible Interpretations in both the *Christian Science Magazine,* at her Seminary and in the *Chicago Inter-Ocean Newspaper.*

First Series

July 5 - September 27, 1891

Lesson 1	The Word Made Flesh *John 1:1-18*	July 5th
Lesson 2	Christ's First Disciples John 1:29-42	July 12th
Lesson 3	All Is Divine Order *John 2:1-1*1 (Christ's first Miracle)	July 19th
Lesson 4	Jesus Christ and Nicodemus *John 3:1-17*	July 26th
Lesson 5	Christ at Samaria *John 4:5-26* (Christ at Jacob's Well)	August 2nd
Lesson 6	Self-condemnation *John 5:17-30* (Christ's Authority)	August 9th
Lesson 7	Feeding the Starving *John 6:1-14* (The Five Thousand Fed)	August 16th
Lesson 8	The Bread of Life *John 6:26-40* (Christ the Bread of Life)	August 23rd
Lesson 9	The Chief Thought *John 7:31-34* (Christ at the Feast)	August 30th
Lesson 10	Continue the Work *John 8:31-47*	September 6th
Lesson 11	Inheritance of Sin *John 9:1-11, 35-38* (Christ and the Blind Man)	September 13th
Lesson 12	The Real Kingdom *John 10:1-16* (Christ the Good Shepherd)	September 20th
Lesson 13	In Retrospection Review	September 27th

Second Series

October 4 - December 27, 1891

Lesson 1	Mary and Martha *John 11:21-44*	October 4th
Lesson 2	Glory of Christ *John 12:20-36*	October 11th
Lesson 3	Good in Sacrifice *John 13:1-17*	October 18th
Lesson 4	Power of the Mind *John 14:13; 15-27*	October 25th
Lesson 5	Vines and Branches *John 15:1-16*	November 1st
Lesson 6	Your Idea of God *John 16:1-15*	November 8th
Lesson 7	Magic of His Name *John 17:1-19*	November 15th
Lesson 8	Jesus and Judas *John 18:1-13*	November 22nd
Lesson 9	Scourge of Tongues *John 19:1-16*	November 29th
Lesson 10	Simplicity of Faith *John 19:17-30*	December 6th
Lesson 11	Christ is All in All *John 20: 1-18*	December 13th
Lesson 12	Risen With Christ *John 21:1-14*	December 20th
Lesson 13	The Spirit is Able Review of Year	December 27th

Third Series

January 3 - March 27, 1892

Lesson 1	A Golden Promise *Isaiah 11:1-10*	January 3rd
Lesson 2	The Twelve Gates *Isaiah 26:1-10*	January 10th
Lesson 3	Who Are Drunkards *Isaiah 28:1-13*	January 17th
Lesson 4	Awake Thou That Sleepest *Isaiah 37:1-21*	January 24th
Lesson 5	The Healing Light *Isaiah 53:1-21*	January 31st
Lesson 6	True Ideal of God *Isaiah 55:1-13*	February 7th
Lesson 7	Heaven Around Us *Jeremiah 31 14-37*	February 14th
Lesson 8	But One Substance *Jeremiah 36:19-31*	February 21st
Lesson 9	Justice of Jehovah *Jeremiah 37:11-21*	February 28th
Lesson 10	God and Man Are One *Jeremiah 39:1-10*	March 6th
Lesson 11	Spiritual Ideas *Ezekiel 4:9, 36:25-38*	March 13th
Lesson 12	All Flesh is Grass *Isaiah 40:1-10*	March 20th
Lesson 13	The Old and New Contrasted Review	March 27th

Fourth Series

April 3 - June 26, 1892

Lesson 1	Realm of Thought *Psalm 1:1-6*	April 3rd
Lesson 2	The Power of Faith *Psalm 2:1-12*	April 10th
Lesson 3	Let the Spirit Work *Psalm 19:1-14*	April 17th
Lesson 4	Christ is Dominion *Psalm 23:1-6*	April 24th
Lesson 5	External or Mystic *Psalm 51:1-13*	May 1st
Lesson 6	Value of Early Beliefs *Psalm 72:1-9*	May 8th
Lesson 7	Truth Makes Free *Psalm 84:1-12*	May 15th
Lesson 8	False Ideas of God *Psalm 103:1-22*	May 22nd
Lesson 9	But Men Must Work *Daniel 1:8-21*	May 29th
Lesson 10	Artificial Helps *Daniel 2:36-49*	June 5th
Lesson 11	Dwelling in Perfect Life *Daniel 3:13-25*	June 12th
Lesson 12	Which Streak Shall Rule *Daniel 6:16-28*	June 19th
Lesson 13	See Things as They Are Review of 12 Lessons	June 26th

Fifth Series

July 3 - September 18, 1892

Lesson 1	The Measure of a Master *Acts 1:1-12*	July 3rd
Lesson 2	Chief Ideas Rule People *Acts 2:1-12*	July 10th
Lesson 3	New Ideas About Healing *Acts 2:37-47*	July 17th
Lesson 4	Heaven a State of Mind *Acts 3:1-16*	July 24th
Lesson 5	About Mesmeric Powers *Acts 4:1-18*	July 31st
Lesson 6	Points in the Mosaic Law *Acts 4:19-31*	August 7th
Lesson 7	Napoleon's Ambition *Acts 5:1-11*	August 14th
Lesson 8	A River Within the Heart *Acts 5:25-41*	August 21st
Lesson 9	The Answering of Prayer Acts 7: 54-60 - Acts 8: 1-4	August 28th
Lesson 10	Words Spoken by the Mind *Acts 8:5-35*	September 4th
Lesson 11	Just What It Teaches Us *Acts 8:26-40*	September 11th
Lesson 12	The Healing Principle Review	September 18th

Sixth Series

September 25 - December 18, 1892

Lesson 1	The Science of Christ *1 Corinthians 11:23-34*	September 25th
Lesson 2	On the Healing of Saul *Acts 9:1-31*	October 2nd
Lesson 3	The Power of the Mind Explained *Acts 9:32-43*	October 9th
Lesson 4	Faith in Good to Come *Acts 10:1-20*	October 16th
Lesson 5	Emerson's Great Task *Acts 10:30-48*	October 23rd
Lesson 6	The Teaching of Freedom *Acts 11:19-30*	October 30th
Lesson 7	Seek and Ye Shall Find *Acts 12:1-17*	November 6th
Lesson 8	The Ministry of the Holy Mother *Acts 13:1-13*	November 13th
Lesson 9	The Power of Lofty Ideas *Acts 13:26-43*	November 20th
Lesson 10	Sure Recipe for Old Age *Acts 13:44-52, 14:1-7*	November 27th
Lesson 11	The Healing Principle *Acts 14:8-22*	December 4th
Lesson 12	Washington's Vision *Acts 15:12-29*	December 11th
Lesson 13	Review of the Quarter Partial Lesson Shepherds and the Star	December 18th December 25th

Seventh Series

January 1 - March 31, 1893

Lesson 1	All is as Allah Wills *Ezra 1*	January 1st
Lesson 2	Zerubbabel's High Ideal *Ezra 2:8-13*	January 8th
Lesson 3	Divine Rays Of Power *Ezra 4*	January 15th
Lesson 4	Visions Of Zechariah *Zechariah 3*	January 22nd
Lesson 5	Spirit of the Land Zechariah 4:1-10	January 27th
Lesson 6	Dedicating the Temple Ezra 6:14-22	February 3rd
Lesson 7	Nehemiah's Prayer *Nehemiah 13*	February 12th
Lesson 8	Ancient Religions *Nehemiah 4*	February 19th
Lesson 9	Understanding is Strength Part 1 *Nehemiah 13*	February 26th
Lesson 10	Understanding is Strength Part 2 *Nehemiah 13*	March 3rd
Lesson 11	Way of the Spirit *Esther*	March 10th
Lesson 12	Speaking of Right Things Proverbs 23:15-23	March 17th
Lesson 13	Review	March 24th

Eighth Series

April 2 - June 25, 1893

Lesson 1	The Resurrection of Christ *Matthew 28:1-10*	April 2nd
Lesson 2	Universal Energy *Book of Job, Part 1*	April 9th
Lesson 3	Strength From Confidence *Book of Job, Part II*	April 16th
Lesson 4	The New Doctrine Brought Out *Book of Job, Part III*	April 23rd
Lesson 5	Wisdom's Warning *Proverbs 1:20-23*	April 30th
Lesson 6	The Law of Understanding *Proverbs 3*	May 7th
Lesson 7	Self-Esteem *Proverbs 12:1-15*	May 14th
Lesson 8	Physical vs. Spiritual Power *Proverbs 23:29-35*	May 21st
Lesson 9	Only One Power (information taken from Review)	May 28th
Lesson 10	Recognizing Our Spiritual Nature *Proverbs 31:10-31*	June 4th
Lesson 11	Intuition *Ezekiel 8:2-3, Ezekiel 9:3-6, 11*	June 11th
Lesson 12	The Power of Faith *Malachi*	June 18th
Lesson 13	Review of the 2nd Quarter *Proverbs 31:10-31*	June 25th

Ninth Series

July 2 - September 27, 1893

Lesson 1	Secret of all Power *Acts 16: 6-15*	July 2nd
Lesson 2	The Flame of Spiritual Verity *Acts 16:18*	July 9th
Lesson 3	Healing Energy Gifts *Acts 18:19-21*	July 16th
Lesson 4	Be Still My Soul *Acts 17:16-24*	July 23rd
Lesson 5	(Missing) Acts 18:1-11	July 30th
Lesson 6	Missing No Lesson *	August 6th
Lesson 7	The Comforter is the Holy Ghost *Acts 20*	August 13th
Lesson 8	Conscious of a Lofty Purpose *Acts 21*	August 20th
Lesson 9	Measure of Understanding *Acts 24:19-32*	August 27th
Lesson 10	The Angels of Paul *Acts 23:25-26*	September 3rd
Lesson 11	The Hope of Israel *Acts 28:20-31*	September 10th
Lesson 12	Joy in the Holy Ghost *Romans 14*	September 17th
Lesson 13	Review *Acts 26-19-32*	September 24th

Tenth Series

October 1 – December 24, 1893

Lesson 1	When the Truth is Known *Romans 1:1-19*	October 1st
Lesson 2	Justification, free grace, redemption *Romans 3:19-26*	October 8th.
Lesson 3	Justification by Faith *Romans 5:1-11* *Romans 12:1-15*	October 15th
Lesson 4	Christian Living *Romans 12:1*	October 22nd
Lesson 5	Comments on the Golden Text *I Corinthians 8:1-13*	October 29th
Lesson 6	Science of the Christ Principle *I Corinthians 12:1-26*	November 5th
Lesson 7	The Grace of Liberality *II Corinthians 8:1-12*	November 12th
Lesson 8	Imitation of Christ *Ephesians 4:20-32*	November 19th
Lesson 9	The Christian Home *Colossians 3:12-25*	November 26th
Lesson 10	*Grateful Obedience* *James 1:16-27*	December 3rd
Lesson 11	The Heavenly Inheritance *I Peter 1:1-12*	December 10th
Lesson 12	The Glorified Saviour *Revelation 1:9-20*	December 17th
Lesson 13	A Christmas Lesson Matthew 2:1-11	December 24th
Lesson 14	Review	December 31st

Eleventh Series

January 1 – March 25, 1894

Lesson 1	The First Adam *Genesis 1:26-31 & 2:1-3*	January 7th
Lesson 2	Adam's Sin and God's Grace *Genesis 3:1-15*	January 14th
Lesson 3	Cain and Abel *Genesis 4:3-13*	January 21st
Lesson 4	God's Covenant With Noah *Genesis 9:8-17*	January 28th
Lesson 5	Beginning of the Hebrew Nation *Genesis 12:1-9*	February 4th
Lesson 6	God's Covenant With Abram *Genesis 17:1-9*	February 11th
Lesson 7	God's Judgment of Sodom *Genesis 18:22-23*	February 18th
Lesson 8	Trial of Abraham's Faith *Genesis 22:1-13*	February 25th
Lesson 9	Selling the Birthright *Genesis 25:27-34*	March 4th
Lesson 10	Jacob at Bethel *Genesis 28:10-22*	March 11th
Lesson 11	Temperance *Proverbs 20:1-7*	March 18th
Lesson 12	Review and Easter *Mark 16:1-8*	March 25th

Twelfth Series

April 1 – June 24, 1894

Lesson 1	Jacob's Prevailing Prayer *Genesis 24:30, 32:9-12*	April 8th
Lesson 2	Discord in Jacob's Family *Genesis 37:1-11*	April 1st
Lesson 3	Joseph Sold into Egypt *Genesis 37:23-36*	April 15th
Lesson 4	Object Lesson in Genesis *Genesis 41:38-48*	April 22nd
Lesson 5	"With Thee is Fullness of Joy" *Genesis 45:1-15*	April 29th
Lesson 6	Change of Heart *Genesis 50:14-26*	May 6th
Lesson 7	Israel in Egypt *Exodus 1:1-14*	May 13th
Lesson 8	The Childhood of Moses *Exodus 2:1-10*	May 20th
Lesson 9	Moses Sent As A Deliverer *Exodus 3:10-20*	May 27th
Lesson 10	The Passover Instituted *Exodus 12:1-14*	June 3rd
Lesson 11	Passage of the Red Sea *Exodus 14:19-29*	June 10th
Lesson 12	The Woes of the Drunkard *Proverbs 23:29-35*	June 17th
Lesson 13	Review	June 24th

Thirteenth Series

July 1 – September 30, 1894

Lesson 1	The Birth of Jesus *Luke 2:1-16*	July 1st
Lesson 2	Presentation in the Temple *Luke 2:25-38*	July 8th
Lesson 3	Visit of the Wise Men *Matthew 1:2-12*	July 15th
Lesson 4	Flight Into Egypt *Mathew 2:13-23*	July 22nd
Lesson 5	The Youth of Jesus *Luke2:40-52*	July 29th
Lesson 6	The "All is God" Doctrine *Luke 2:40-52*	August 5th
Lesson 7	Missing	August 12th
Lesson 8	First Disciples of Jesus *John 1:36-49*	August 19th
Lesson 9	The First Miracle of Jesus *John 2:1-11*	August 26th
Lesson 10	Jesus Cleansing the Temple *John 2:13-25*	September 2nd
Lesson 11	Jesus and Nicodemus *John 3:1-16*	September 9th
Lesson 12	Jesus at Jacob's Well *John 4:9-26*	September 16th
Lesson 13	Daniel's Abstinence *Daniel 1:8-20*	September 23rd
Lesson 14	Review *John 2:13-25*	September 30th

Fourteenth Series

October 7 – December 30, 1894

Lesson 1	Jesus At Nazareth *Luke 4:16-30*	October 7th
Lesson 2	The Draught of Fishes *Luke 5:1-11*	October 14th
Lesson 3	The Sabbath in Capernaum *Mark 1:21-34*	October 21st
Lesson 4	The Paralytic Healed *Mark 2:1-12*	October 28th
Lesson 5	Reading of Sacred Books *Mark 2:23-38, Mark 3:1-5*	November 4th
Lesson 6	Spiritual Executiveness *Mark 3:6-19*	November 11th
Lesson 7	Twelve Powers Of The Soul *Luke 6:20-31*	November 18th
Lesson 8	Things Not Understood Attributed to Satan *Mark 3:22-35*	November 25th
Lesson 9	Independence of Mind *Luke 7:24-35*	December 2nd
Lesson 10	The Gift of Untaught Wisdom *Luke 8:4-15*	December 9th
Lesson 11	The Divine Eye Within *Matthew 5:5-16*	December 16th
Lesson 12	Unto Us a Child I s Born *Luke 7:24-35*	December 23rd
Lesson 13	Review *Isaiah 9:2-7*	December 30th

Fifteenth Series

January 6-March 31, 1895

Lesson 1	Missing	January 6th
	Mark 6:17-29	
Lesson 2	The Prince Of The World	January 13th
	Mark 6:30-44	
Lesson 3	The Golden Text	January 20th
	John 6:25-35	
Lesson 4	The Golden Text	January 27th
	Matthew 16:13-25	
Lesson 5	The Transfiguration	February 3rd
	Luke 9:28-36	
Lesson 6	Christ And The Children	February 10th
	Matthew 18:1-14	
Lesson 7	The Good Samaritan	February 17th
	Luke 10:25-37	
Lesson 8	Christ And The Man Born Blind	February 24th
	John 9:1-11	
Lesson 9	The Raising Of Lazarus	March 3rd
	John 11:30-45	
Lesson 10	The Rich Young Ruler	March 10th
	Mark 10:17-27	
Lesson 11	Zaccheus The Publican	March 17th
	Luke 1:10	
Lesson 12	Purity Of Life	March 24th
	Romans 13:8-14	
Lesson 13	Review	March 31st

Sixteenth Series

April 7-June 30, 1895

Lesson 1	The Triumphal Entry *Mark 11:1-11*	April 7th
Lesson 2	The Easter Lesson *Mark 12:1-12*	April 14th
Lesson 3	Watchfulness Mark 24:42-51	April 21st
Lesson 4	The Lord's Supper *Mark 14:12-26*	April 28th
Lesson 5	Jesus in Gethsemane Mark 15:42-52	May 5th
Lesson 6	The Jesus Christ Power *Mark 14:53-72*	May 12th
Lesson 7	Jesus Before Pilate *Mark 15:1-15*	May 19th
Lesson 8	The Day of the Crucifixion *Mark 15:22-37*	May 26th
Lesson 9	At the Tomb *Mark 16:1-8*	June 2nd
Lesson 10	The Road To Emmaus *Luke 24:13-32*	June 9th
Lesson 11	Fisher of Men *John 21:4-17*	June 16th
Lesson 12	Missing Luke 24:27-29	June 23rd
Lesson 13	Review	June 30th

Seventeenth Series

July 7 – September 29, 1895

Lesson 1	The Bread of Energy *Exodus 22:1-17*	July 7th
Lesson 2	Grandeur is Messiahship *Exodus 32:30-35*	July 14th
Lesson 3	Temperance *Leviticus 10:1-9*	July 21st
Lesson 4	The Alluring Heart of Man *Numbers 10:29-36*	July 28th
Lesson 5	As a Man Thinketh Numbers 13:17-23	August 4th
Lesson 6	Rock of Eternal Security *Numbers 31:4-9*	August 11th
Lesson 7	Something Behind *Deuteronomy 6:3-15*	August 18th
Lesson 8	What You See Is What You Get *Joshua 3:5-17*	August 25th
Lesson 9	Every Man To His Miracle *Joshua 6:8-20*	September 1st
Lesson 10	Every Man To His Harvest *Joshua 14:5-14*	September 8th
Lesson 11	Every Man To His Refuge *Joshua 20:1-9*	September 15th
Lesson 12	The Twelve Propositions Joshua 24:14-25	September 22nd
Lesson 13	Review I Kings 8:56	September 29th